Daily Words *of* Comfort

LARGE PRINT

Publications International, Ltd.

ISBN: 978-1-64558-757-6

Manufactured in China.

8 7 6 5 4 3 2 1

Let's get social!

⬤ @Publications_International

⬤ @PublicationsInternational

www.pilbooks.com

Contents

Dear God of comfort, I
sense your loving presence all
around me, in the ground be-
neath my feet, in the warming
sun on my shoulders, in the
gentle songs of the birds. You
have made this world for us,
your children, and the sight,
sound, and touch of your
creations comfort me as they
surround me each day.

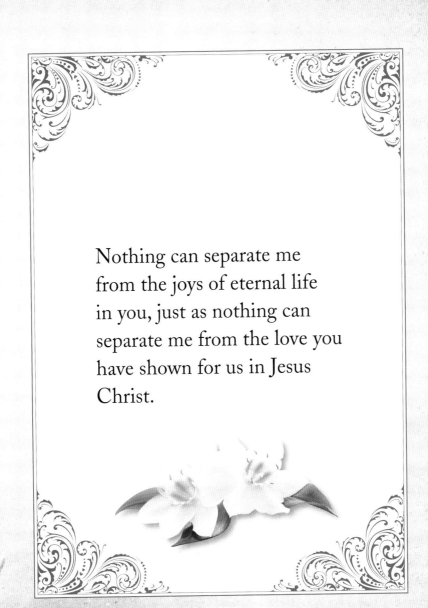

Nothing can separate me
from the joys of eternal life
in you, just as nothing can
separate me from the love you
have shown for us in Jesus
Christ.

January

*Thou art my hiding place
and my shield:
I hope in thy word.*

—Psalm 119:114

Like the evergreen, hope never dies, but
stands tall and mighty against the coldest
winter winds until the summer sun returns
to warm its outstretched branches.

Cause me to hear thy lovingkindness
in the morning;
for in thee do I trust:
cause me to know the way wherein
I should walk;
for I lift up my soul unto thee.

—Psalm 143:8

It is only through the eyes of someone we love that we see who we really are.

The heart that loves is always
young.
—Greek proverb

Honesty,
humility,
generosity,
patience—
four cornerstones of love.

This is my commandment,
That ye love one another,
as I have loved you.

—John 15:12

The path of love is never easy. Yet it is in the ups and downs, the times of trouble and need, that together you forge a bond strong enough to withstand whatever the road ahead may bring.

Lord, how freeing it is to rid our drawers and closets of unneeded clothing and pass it along to someone who can really use it! Thanks for reminding us that since you provide for our needs, we don't need to hold on to any surplus. Keep us mindful that true beauty comes not from the latest fashions but from hearts dedicated to sharing your love with the world.

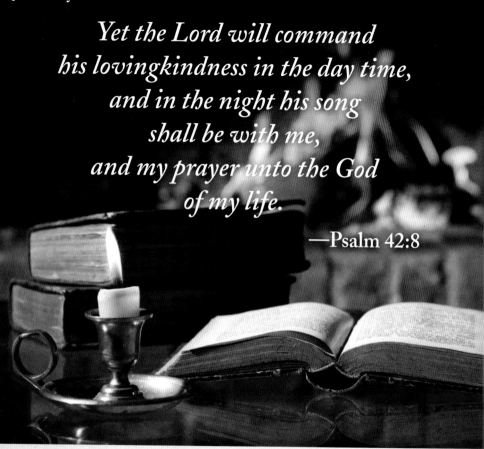

*Yet the Lord will command
his lovingkindness in the day time,
and in the night his song
shall be with me,
and my prayer unto the God
of my life.*

—Psalm 42:8

Loving, like prayer, is a power as well as a process. It's curative. It is creative.
—Zona Gale

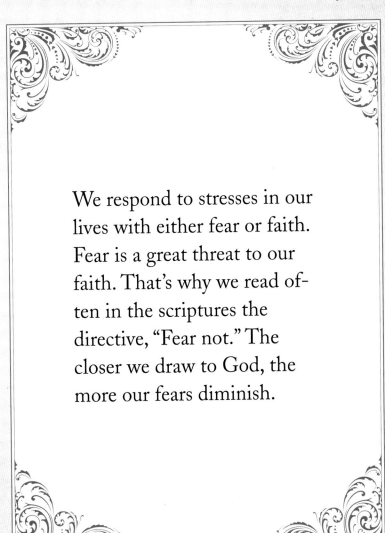

We respond to stresses in our lives with either fear or faith. Fear is a great threat to our faith. That's why we read often in the scriptures the directive, "Fear not." The closer we draw to God, the more our fears diminish.

Comfort me, O God, as I seek shelter from the storms of everyday life. I am grateful for the good I have, but sometimes feel I cannot carry the burden of life's challenges alone. Remind me with your loving presence that no matter what my day brings, you are there for me, with me, and on my behalf, making smooth the way before me. In your love I find rest.

But speaking the truth in love,
may grow up into him in all things,
which is the head, even Christ.

—Ephesians 4:15

Lord, I know that doubts and confusion don't come from you. On days when everything I know to be true is challenged—and I feel like I'm walking through a fog that won't lift—be my source of truth and light. Bring me back to complete trust in you.

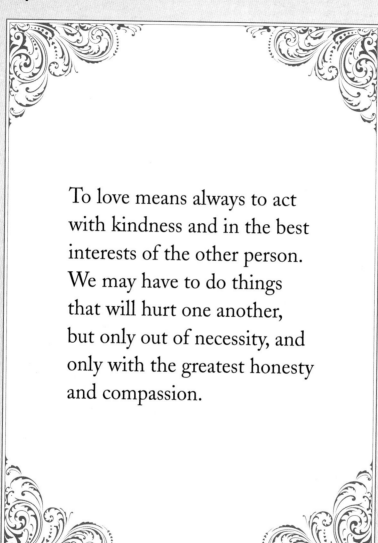

To love means always to act
with kindness and in the best
interests of the other person.
We may have to do things
that will hurt one another,
but only out of necessity, and
only with the greatest honesty
and compassion.

January 11

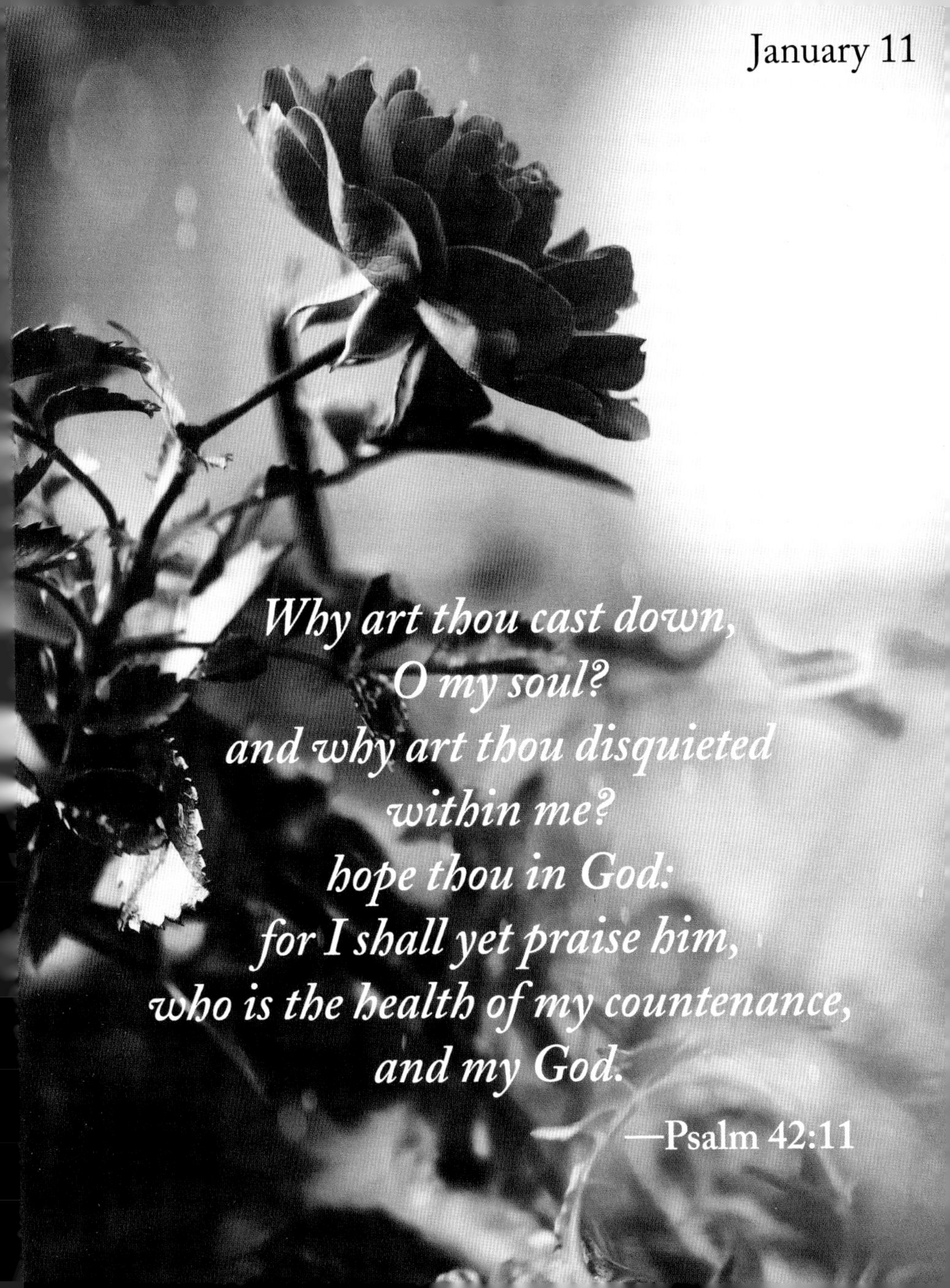

Why art thou cast down,
O my soul?
and why art thou disquieted
within me?
hope thou in God:
for I shall yet praise him,
who is the health of my countenance,
and my God.

—Psalm 42:11

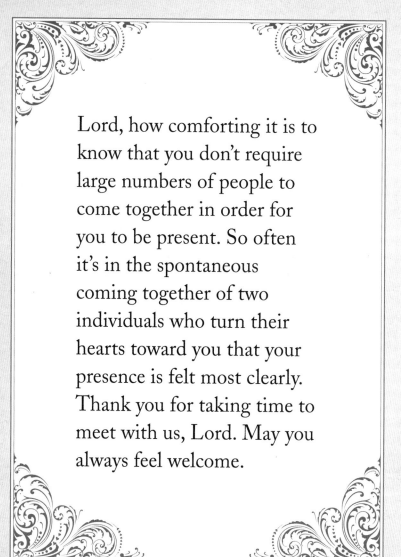

Lord, how comforting it is to know that you don't require large numbers of people to come together in order for you to be present. So often it's in the spontaneous coming together of two individuals who turn their hearts toward you that your presence is felt most clearly. Thank you for taking time to meet with us, Lord. May you always feel welcome.

*Let thy mercy, O Lord, be upon us,
according as we hope in thee.*

—Psalm 33:22

Hope and patience are two sovereign remedies for all, the surest reposals, the softest cushions to lean on in adversity.
—Robert Burton

*I love the Lord, because he hath
heard my voice and my supplications.
Because he hath inclined his
ear unto me, therefore will I call upon
him as long as I live.*

—Psalm 116:1-2

This world is full of people who have to be right, even if it means losing friendships or family connections. The need to be right causes so much suffering. Instead, seek the need to be wise. Seek the ability to use your God-given wisdom to be of help to others, and not a burden. No one is right all the time, and it takes wisdom to realize that and to learn to be compassionate to others, and to yourself.

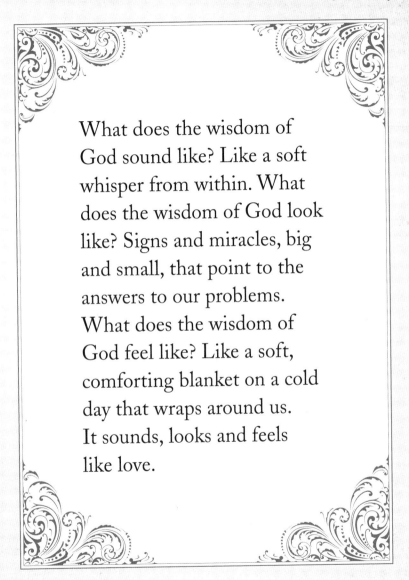

What does the wisdom of God sound like? Like a soft whisper from within. What does the wisdom of God look like? Signs and miracles, big and small, that point to the answers to our problems. What does the wisdom of God feel like? Like a soft, comforting blanket on a cold day that wraps around us. It sounds, looks and feels like love.

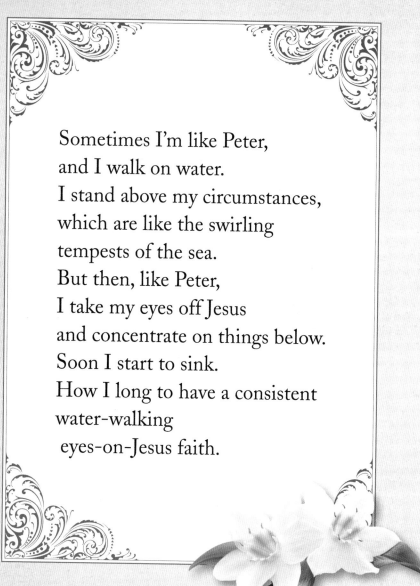

Sometimes I'm like Peter,
and I walk on water.
I stand above my circumstances,
which are like the swirling
tempests of the sea.
But then, like Peter,
I take my eyes off Jesus
and concentrate on things below.
Soon I start to sink.
How I long to have a consistent
water-walking
 eyes-on-Jesus faith.

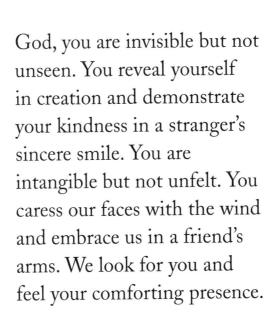

God, you are invisible but not unseen. You reveal yourself in creation and demonstrate your kindness in a stranger's sincere smile. You are intangible but not unfelt. You caress our faces with the wind and embrace us in a friend's arms. We look for you and feel your comforting presence.

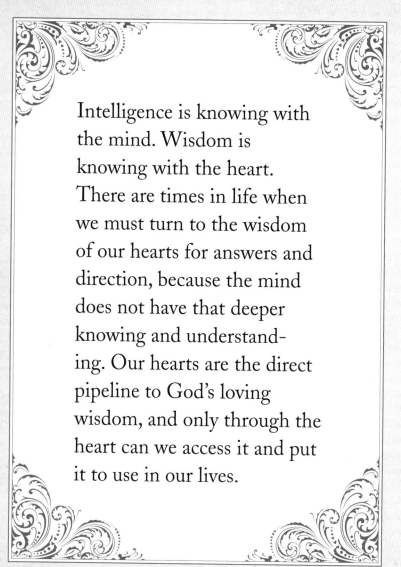

Intelligence is knowing with the mind. Wisdom is knowing with the heart. There are times in life when we must turn to the wisdom of our hearts for answers and direction, because the mind does not have that deeper knowing and understanding. Our hearts are the direct pipeline to God's loving wisdom, and only through the heart can we access it and put it to use in our lives.

Mercy unto you, and peace, and love, be multiplied.

—Jude 1:2

Heavenly Father, when I was young, I thought all things hurt or broken could be fixed: knees, feelings, bicycles, tea sets. Now I've learned that not everything can be repaired, relieved, or cured. As a mother comforts her child, heal my hurting and grant me the peace I used to know. This I pray. Amen.

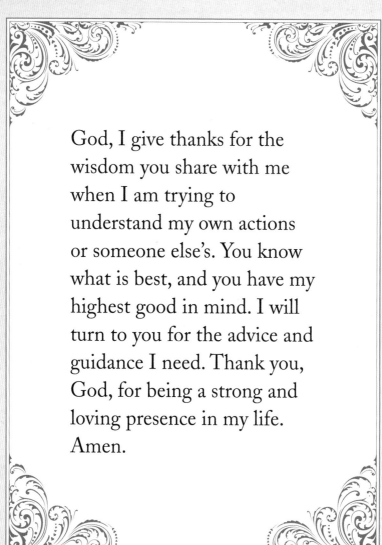

God, I give thanks for the wisdom you share with me when I am trying to understand my own actions or someone else's. You know what is best, and you have my highest good in mind. I will turn to you for the advice and guidance I need. Thank you, God, for being a strong and loving presence in my life. Amen.

Love is greater than faith, because the end is greater than the means. What is the use of having faith? It is to connect the soul to God. And what is the object of connecting man with God? That he may become like God. But God is love. Hence, faith, the means, is in order to love, the end. Love, therefore, obviously is greater than faith. "If I have all faith, so as to remove mountains, but have not love, I am nothing."
—Henry Drummond

Holy God, you have shown me light and life. You are stronger than any natural power. Accept the words from my heart that struggle to reach you. Accept the silent thoughts and feelings that are offered to you. Clear my mind of the clutter of useless facts. Bend down to me, and lift me in your arms. Make me holy as you are holy. Give me a voice to sing of your love to others.

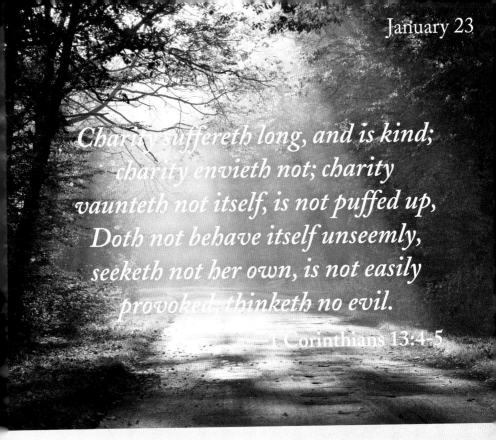

Charity suffereth long, and is kind; charity envieth not; charity vaunteth not itself, is not puffed up, Doth not behave itself unseemly, seeketh not her own, is not easily provoked, thinketh no evil.

—I Corinthians 13:4-5

Stand in a beloved's shade, not shadow, and discover new sights to share, new directions to go, all leading to even more reasons for standing together.

*So shall the knowledge of wisdom
be unto thy soul:
when thou hast found it,
then there shall be a reward,
and thy expectation shall
not be cut off.*

—Proverbs 24:14

What we cannot do for ourselves, God can do for us. With our limited vision and perception, only God's wisdom can look beyond our lack and limitations. How comforting is it to know that we have this resource to turn to anytime we need? God is always ready to help us, to advise us, and to direct us.

When I am wrong, I turn
within to find the right way.
God's eternal wisdom is like
a flowing river I can tap into
at any time, especially when
I am clueless and don't know
which way to turn. I take
comfort in knowing I don't
have to be a genius and
figure out every last detail of
my life. God knows best, and
as long as I stay in tune with
his word, I will surely be
divinely inspired.

Almighty God, why is it we don't remember that you alone are the source of all comfort? Instead, when times are tough, we seek comfort in the things of the world that we see around us—in too much food, or drink, or late-night television. Those things can distract us, but we know they can never comfort us the way you do. Thank you for your faithfulness, God. For at the end of every one of our fruitless searches you are there, and in your presence we find true comfort.

Love comforts, never alarms;
Always heals, never harms.
Always grows, never diminishes;
Love begins, never finishes.

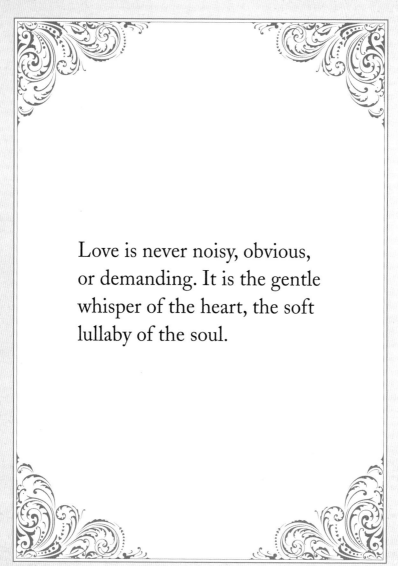

Love is never noisy, obvious, or demanding. It is the gentle whisper of the heart, the soft lullaby of the soul.

Comforting God, blessed is your presence. For you and you alone give me power to walk through dark valleys into the light again. You and you alone give me hope when there seems no end to my suffering. You and you alone give me peace when the noise of my life overwhelms me. I ask that you give this same power, hope, and peace to all who know discouragement, that they, too, may be emboldened and renewed by your everlasting love.

Lord, this aloneness is almost more than
I can take! If I could escape in a good
night's sleep, I would. But my thoughts
and fears and emotions are restless,
hovering around this center of heartache.
If it were not for you being here with me,
I would despair. But your quiet presence
keeps me from unraveling. These nights,
these long drawn out nights of solitude,
are where I find you waiting, ready to
speak comfort to my heart and assure
me that you have a future in store for me
that is good and worth waiting for.
Tonight, even if sleep eludes me again,
I'll continue to rest in your love for me.

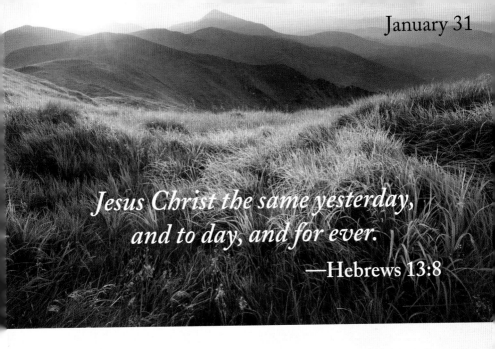

Jesus Christ the same yesterday, and to day, and for ever.

—Hebrews 13:8

Always
I may not call to talk with you as often as I should.
I may not come to visit you as often as I could.
And even though our busy lives sometimes keep us apart,
no matter how much time goes by, you're always in my heart.

February

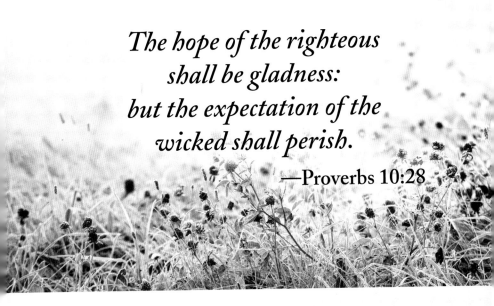

> *The hope of the righteous*
> *shall be gladness:*
> *but the expectation of the*
> *wicked shall perish.*
>
> —Proverbs 10:28

Oh, men and women of riper years, let us
not fail to carry our earlier enthusiasms
into the dry details, the grave
responsibilities of later life and make
the desert places rejoice and blossom
as the rose!
—Charles Sumner Hoyt, *The Octave of Life*
(1901)

And beside this, giving all diligence, add to your faith virtue; and to virtue knowledge; And to knowledge temperance; and to temperance patience; and to patience godliness; And to godliness brotherly kindness; and to brotherly kindness charity.

—2 Peter 1:5-7

Faith is knowing without seeing, believing without fully understanding, trusting without touching the One who is ever faithful.

And he answering said, Thou shalt love the Lord thy God with all thy heart, and with all thy soul, and with all thy strength, and with all thy mind; and thy neighbour as thyself.

—Luke 10:27

The best way to deal with the pressures of everyday life is to patiently rely on God.

God hears my cries for help, and
he answers every prayer.
I only need be patient—
He supplies the "how"
and "where."

Sometimes it may be immediate
in a tangible way I'll know;
while other times I wait assured
that he is strengthening my soul.

His grace is all-sufficient
to meet my heart-cries need.
As I lean upon his promises,
walking in faith, he'll lead.

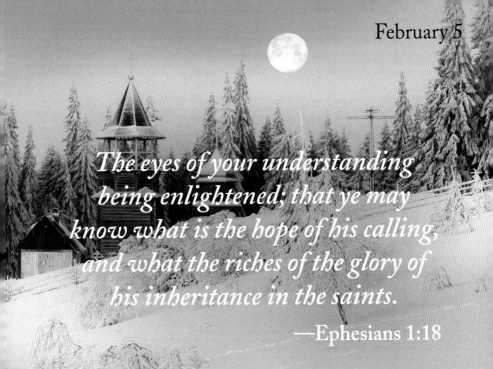

The eyes of your understanding being enlightened; that ye may know what is the hope of his calling, and what the riches of the glory of his inheritance in the saints.

—Ephesians 1:18

Forgiveness is the soil in which God nurtures our emotional healing and our ability to love once again.
—John Nieder and Thomas M. Thompson

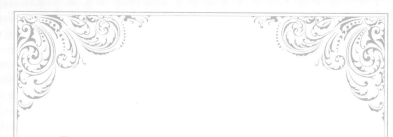

Peace in the family is the consciousness that, under all the strains inevitably incident to the running of a home, there is an unfailing wealth of love and devotion and fidelity to fall back upon. Peace in the soul is the consciousness that, however difficult life may be, we are not living it alone...
—Harry Emerson Fosdick

Hope deferred maketh the heart sick:
but when the desire cometh,
it is a tree of life.

—Proverbs 13:12

Sometimes we believe our souls can only
be at peace if there is no outer turmoil.
The wonder of God's peace is that even
when the world around us is in confusion
and our emotions are in a whirl,
underneath it all we can know his peace.

We cannot tell how often as
we pray
  For some bewildered one,
hurt and distressed,
The answer comes, but many
times these hearts
  Find sudden peace and rest.
Someone had prayed, and
faith, a lifted hand
  Reached up to God, and
He reached down that day.
So many, many hearts have
need of prayer—
  Then, let us, let us pray.
—Harry Emerson Fosdick

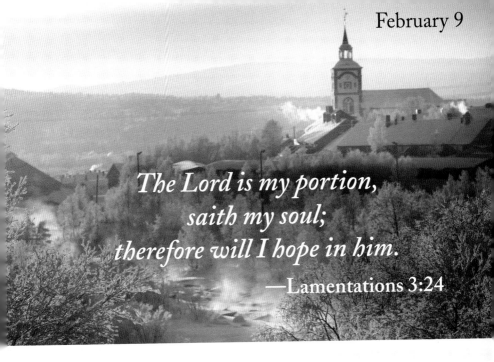

*The Lord is my portion,
saith my soul;
therefore will I hope in him.*

—Lamentations 3:24

If we are devoted to the cause of humanity, we shall soon be crushed and broken-hearted...but if our motive is love to God, no ingratitude can hinder us from serving our fellow men.

—Oswald Chambers

Lead me in thy truth, and teach me:
for thou art the God of my salvation;
on thee do I wait all the day.

—Psalm 25:5

There are many events in our lives over which we have no control. However, we do have a choice either to endure trying times and press on or to give up. The secret of survival, whether or not we question God's presence or his ability to help us, is remembering that our hope is in the fairness, goodness, and justice of God. When we put our trust in the character of a God who cannot fail us, we will remain faithful. Our trust and faithfulness produce the endurance that sees us through the "tough stuff" we all face in this life.

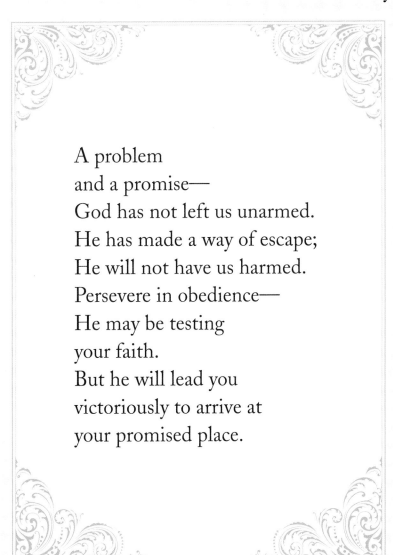

A problem
and a promise—
God has not left us unarmed.
He has made a way of escape;
He will not have us harmed.
Persevere in obedience—
He may be testing
your faith.
But he will lead you
victoriously to arrive at
your promised place.

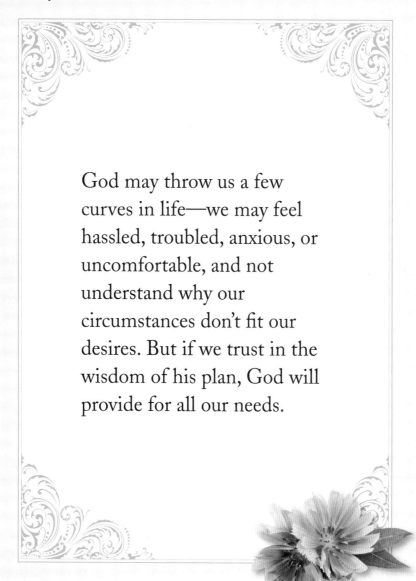

God may throw us a few curves in life—we may feel hassled, troubled, anxious, or uncomfortable, and not understand why our circumstances don't fit our desires. But if we trust in the wisdom of his plan, God will provide for all our needs.

Wisdom is the ability to meet each situation with discernment and good judgment, whether in dealing with others, making choices, or dispensing justice. Wisdom involves using the knowledge we have to take the proper course of action—if we know and don't act, it is the same as not knowing at all. When we let Christ become the source of our wisdom, he will guide us in making wise decisions and acting on them.

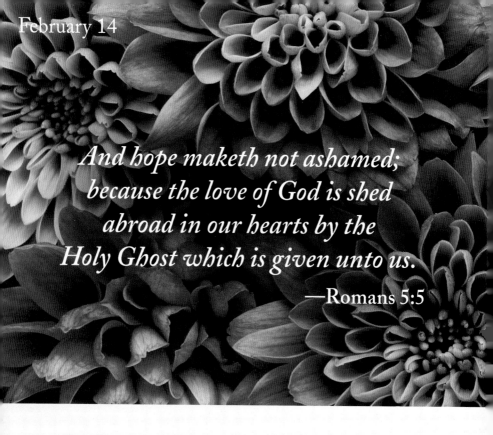

And hope maketh not ashamed;
because the love of God is shed
abroad in our hearts by the
Holy Ghost which is given unto us.

—Romans 5:5

To live a life of faith is to live always in
God's comforting presence, at peace
in the home of his love.

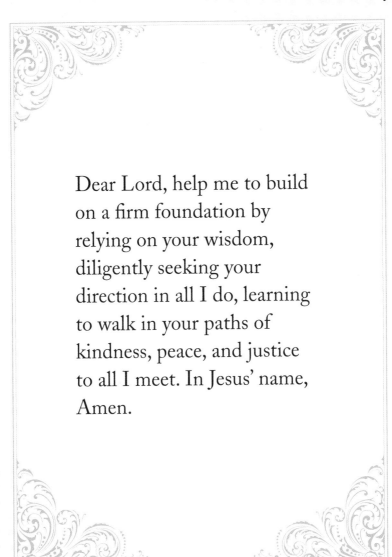

Dear Lord, help me to build
on a firm foundation by
relying on your wisdom,
diligently seeking your
direction in all I do, learning
to walk in your paths of
kindness, peace, and justice
to all I meet. In Jesus' name,
Amen.

As a nation we are indebted to the Book of books for our national ideas and representative institutions. Their preservation rests in adhering to its principles.
—Herbert Hoover

When we really want to acquire wisdom, we must start by getting to know God better.

Follow peace with all men, and holiness, without which no man shall see the Lord.

—Hebrews 12:14

To live a life of faith is to live always in God's presence, at peace in the home of his love.

*Be of good courage, and he shall
strengthen your heart,
all ye that hope in the Lord.*

—Psalm 31:24

It takes great courage to heal, Lord, great
energy to reach out from this darkness to
touch the hem of your garment and ask
for healing. Bless the brave voices telling
nightmare tales of dreadful wounds to the
gifted healers of this world. Together,
sufferers and healers are binding up
damaged parts and laying down burdens
carried so long.

There is one body, and one Spirit, even as ye are called in one hope of your calling.

—Ephesians 4:4

Remember to turn to God for help, for in him there is rescue, refuge, and peace.

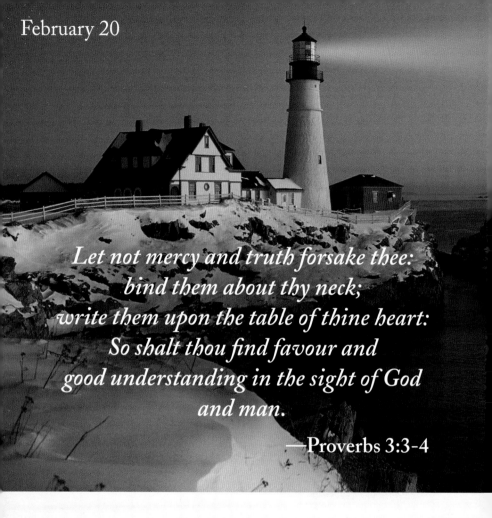

*Let not mercy and truth forsake thee:
bind them about thy neck;
write them upon the table of thine heart:
So shalt thou find favour and
good understanding in the sight of God
and man.*

—Proverbs 3:3-4

Faith preserves a truth that lies beyond
our field of vision—a truth only our hearts
have eyes to see.

In the midst of the darkness
that threatens to overwhelm
us lies a pinpoint of light, a
persistent flicker that guides
us through the pain and fear,
through the hopelessness and
despair, to a place of peace
and healing on the other side.
This is God's spirit, leading
us back home like the
lighthouse beacon that directs
the ships through the fog to
the safety of the harbor.

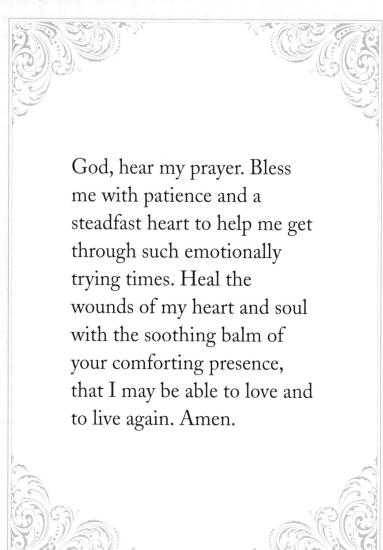

God, hear my prayer. Bless me with patience and a steadfast heart to help me get through such emotionally trying times. Heal the wounds of my heart and soul with the soothing balm of your comforting presence, that I may be able to love and to live again. Amen.

For God hath not given us the spirit of fear; but of power, and of love, and of a sound mind.

—2 Timothy 1:7

Having knowledge is not the same as having wisdom. The true test of wisdom is knowing how and when to act, according to God's will.

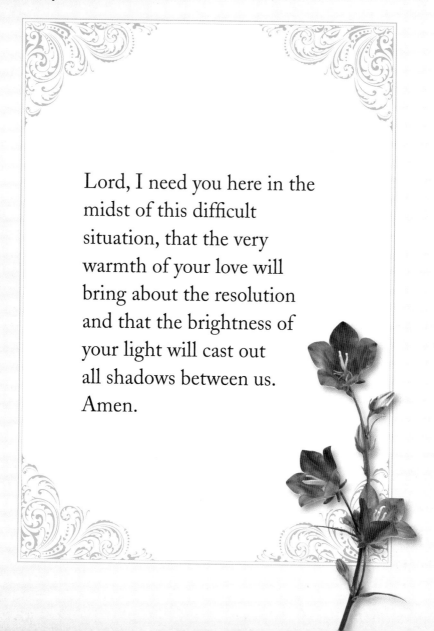

Lord, I need you here in the midst of this difficult situation, that the very warmth of your love will bring about the resolution and that the brightness of your light will cast out all shadows between us. Amen.

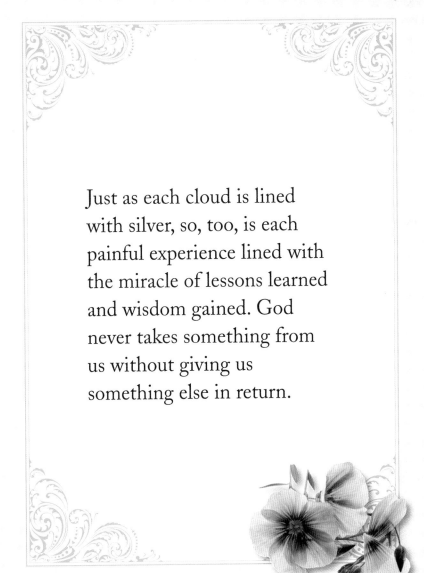

Just as each cloud is lined
with silver, so, too, is each
painful experience lined with
the miracle of lessons learned
and wisdom gained. God
never takes something from
us without giving us
something else in return.

He is a loving, tender hand, full of sympathy and compassion.

—Dwight L. Moody

God of my heart, I am a broken person. I do not know how to handle this suffering. I am not strong enough to do it alone. Be my strength, God, and do for me what I simply cannot do for myself. Be the glue that binds the pieces of my shattered soul back together, that I may rise and step back onto the joyful path of life again. Amen.

Is illness your will, Lord? I need answers, for I want you to help me heal. But if you send illness, how can I trust you to heal? Reassure me that you will work everything out eventually. And when that isn't possible, be with me as I suffer. Freed from fear I can get stronger as your healing energy flows through me, restoring me to my abundant life.

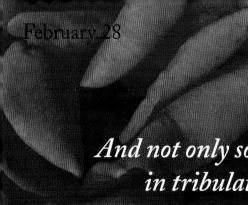

*And not only so, but we glory
in tribulations also:
knowing that tribulation worketh
patience; And patience, experience;
and experience, hope.*

—Romans 5:3-4

I have such good intentions, Lord of promise, but sometimes I slip in carrying them out. Guide my actions so that they match my words as I make footprints for my children to follow. Make me worthy of being a pathfinder. Amen.

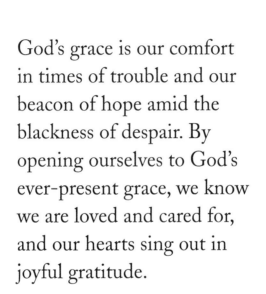

God's grace is our comfort
in times of trouble and our
beacon of hope amid the
blackness of despair. By
opening ourselves to God's
ever-present grace, we know
we are loved and cared for,
and our hearts sing out in
joyful gratitude.

March

...in all human sorrows nothing gives comfort but love and faith.

—Leo Tolstoy,

Anna Karenina

Oh Lord, I do not know how to deal with this person. I am afraid and angry, and my heart aches with sadness. I turn to you, God, and ask for the peace that passes all understanding. I surrender the yoke of my burden to you, that your will be done, not mine. Let me rest in the healing waters of your ever-present spirit, now and forever. Amen.

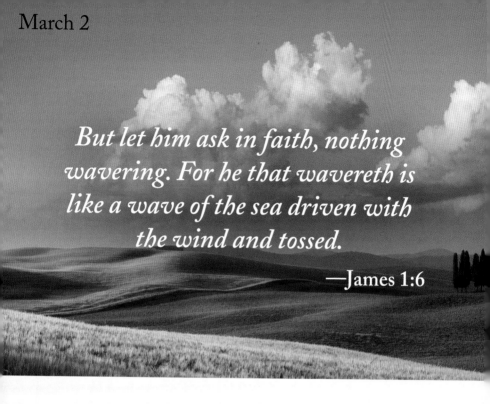

But let him ask in faith, nothing wavering. For he that wavereth is like a wave of the sea driven with the wind and tossed.

—James 1:6

A wise person accepts the help she is offered. A foolish person swears she'll do it herself. A wise person shows gratitude. A foolish person needs glory. A wise person dances with the rhythm of her angels. A foolish person trudges to nobody's drum.

The greatest good is wisdom.

—St. Augustine

If you find stumbling blocks in your path, use them as stepping stones to move closer to the good in life.

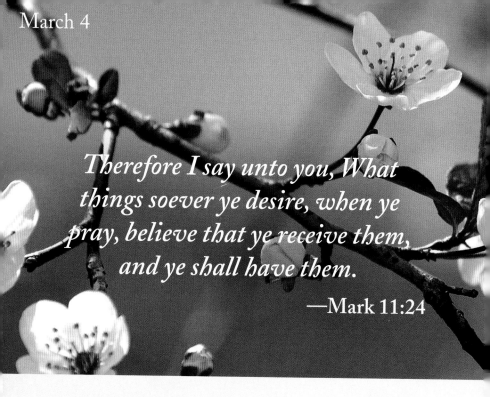

Therefore I say unto you, What things soever ye desire, when ye pray, believe that ye receive them, and ye shall have them.

—Mark 11:24

Dear Lord and Father of humankind,
forgive our foolish ways;
reclothe us in our rightful mind,
in purer lives thy service find,
in deeper reverence, praise.
—John Greenleaf Whittier

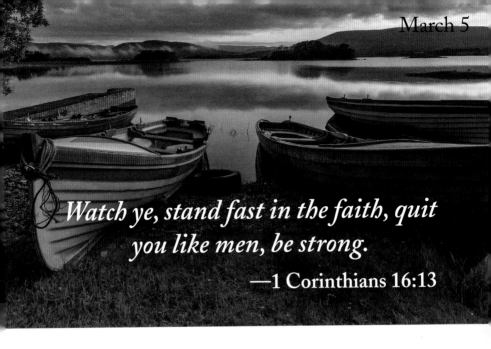

Watch ye, stand fast in the faith, quit you like men, be strong.

—1 Corinthians 16:13

It seems so insignificant,
this choice you have to make.
Yet the Lord can use small acts of faith
to cause the earth to shake!
So pray and wait to know his will
for decisions made today,
and the Lord may use your faithfulness
to show someone the way.

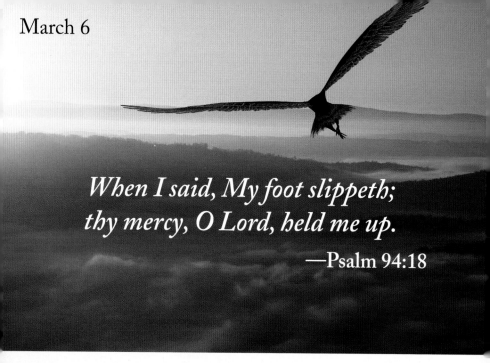

When I said, My foot slippeth;
thy mercy, O Lord, held me up.

—Psalm 94:18

May he support us all the day long, till
the shades lengthen, and the evening
comes, and the busy world is hushed,
and the fever of life is over, and our work
is done! Then in his mercy may he give us
a safe lodging, and a holy rest, and peace
at the last.

—John Henry Newman

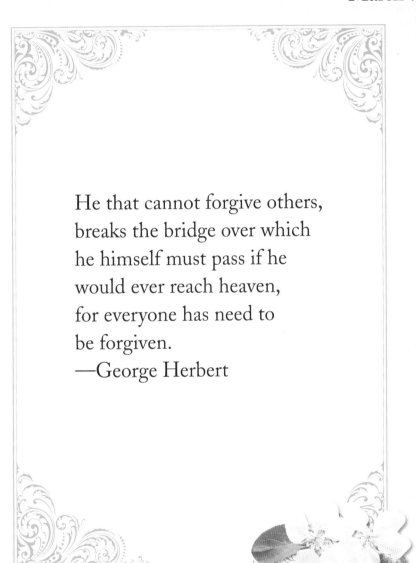

He that cannot forgive others,
breaks the bridge over which
he himself must pass if he
would ever reach heaven,
for everyone has need to
be forgiven.
—George Herbert

*The Lord is merciful and gracious,
slow to anger, and plenteous in mercy.*

—Psalm 103:8

Sometimes when we feel like no one is on
our side, we have to remind ourselves that
no matter what obstacles of life crowd our
path, we are never abandoned without an
angel walking beside us.

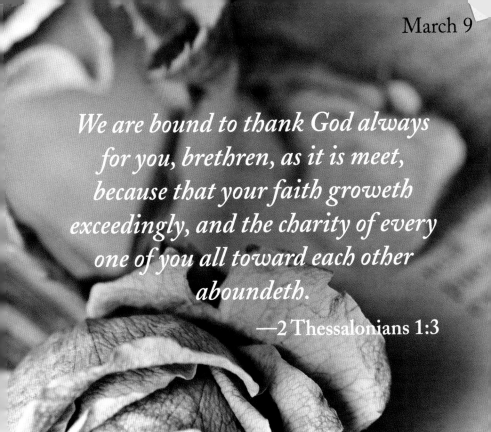

We are bound to thank God always for you, brethren, as it is meet, because that your faith groweth exceedingly, and the charity of every one of you all toward each other aboundeth.

—2 Thessalonians 1:3

We have but faith: we cannot know;
for knowledge is of things we see;
and yet we trust it comes from thee,
a beam in darkness: let it grow.
—Alfred, Lord Tennyson

Count neither the hours nor
the seconds that filled your
mind with doubts and fears.
Do not add up unhappy mo-
ments, when pain and hardships
brought you to tears. Regard
not days on faded calendars
that marked the passage of your
years. Instead, count heaven's
blessings... Grandchildren play-
ing on the floor, old friends
walking through the door,
white clouds drifting up above,
and, like a faithful timepiece,
God's love.

For I say, through the grace given unto me, to every man that is among you, not to think of himself more highly than he ought to think; but to think soberly, according as God hath dealt to every man the measure of faith.

—Romans 12:3

Faith is a living, daring confidence in God's grace. It is so sure and certain that a man could stake his life on it a thousand times.
—Martin Luther

This is our darkest hour when
we feel we cannot suffer any
worse. Yet, something inside
whispers to us, "For everything there is a season," and
we notice the faint glimmer
of hope at the end of this
long, dark tunnel of despair.
The more we seek the light,
the brighter it becomes. This
is God's love and compassion
for us making itself known,
and in his growing presence,
we become stronger and our
faith is renewed.

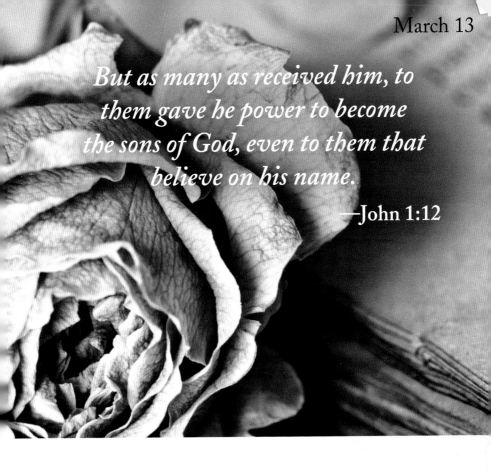

But as many as received him, to them gave he power to become the sons of God, even to them that believe on his name.

—John 1:12

Angels help us believe in those things we can't see and understand those things we can. Angels give us the gifts of faith and wisdom to know all things are possible.

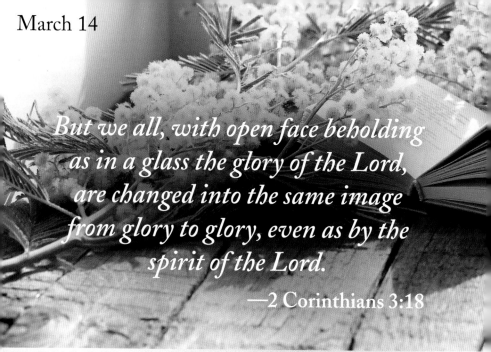

*But we all, with open face beholding
as in a glass the glory of the Lord,
are changed into the same image
from glory to glory, even as by the
spirit of the Lord.*

—2 Corinthians 3:18

Far better it is to dare mighty things,
to win glorious triumphs, even though
checkered by failure, than to take rank
with those poor spirits who neither enjoy
much nor suffer much, because they live
in the gray twilight that knows not victory
nor defeat.
—Theodore Roosevelt

Gratitude is an attitude of loving what you have, and this undoubtedly leads to having even more. When you open your eyes to the bountiful blessings already in your life, you realize just how abundant the world really is. Suddenly, you feel more giving, more loving, and more open to even greater blessings. Gratitude is a key that unlocks the door to treasures you already have, and it yields greater treasures yet to be discovered.

*Every man according as he
purposeth in his heart, so let him
give; not grudgingly, or of necessity:
for God loveth a cheerful giver.*

—2 Corinthians 9:7

He leadeth me O blessed thought,
O words with heavenly comfort fraught,
whate'er I do, where'er I be,
still 'tis God's hand that leadeth me.
—Joseph Henry Gilmore

And though I have the gift of prophecy, and understand all mysteries, and all knowledge; and though I have all faith, so that I could remove mountains, and have not charity, I am nothing.

—1 Corinthians 13:2

God, please remind me throughout my day that the moment is all I have in which to live. I can't retrieve or retract anything I've done or said just ten minutes ago. Nor can I be sure of what will happen ten minutes hence. So I pray, Lord, help me leave the past and the future with you so that I can experience the peace of your love in this important bit of eternity called "now."

85

Abide with me,
fast falls the eventide;
the darkness deepens;
Lord, with me abide!
When other helpers fail
and comforts flee,
help of the helpless,
o abide with me.
I need thy presence
every passing hour;
what but thy grace
can foil the tempter's power?
Who like thyself,
my guide and stay can be?
Through cloud and sunshine,
Lord, abide, with me.

—Henry F. Lyte

The Lord bless thee, and keep thee:
The Lord make his face shine upon
thee, and be gracious unto thee:
The Lord lift up his countenance
upon thee, and give thee peace.

—Numbers 6:24-26

Before me peaceful,
behind me peaceful,
under me peaceful,
over me peaceful,
all around me peaceful.

Disaster can strike at any time without warning to anyone anywhere. Our lives can change dramatically in one unexpected moment, but in the worst times of our lives, we can lean on family, friends, and even strangers who reach out to us. Yet, even more importantly, we can turn to God, who is always there for us during our darkest hours. He will never fail us, never let us down, and never turn away from us when we cry out to him.

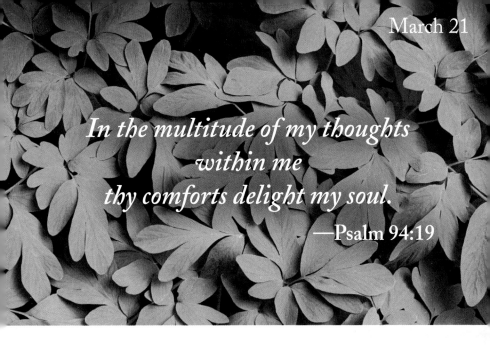

*In the multitude of my thoughts
within me
thy comforts delight my soul.*

—Psalm 94:19

Joy is love expected;
peace is love in repose;
long-suffering is love enduring;
gentleness is love in society;
goodness is love in action;
faith is love on the battlefield;
meekness is love in school;
and temperance is love in training.
—Dwight L. Moody

*But they that wait upon the Lord
shall renew their strength;
they shall mount up with wings as
eagles; they shall run, and not be
weary; and they shall walk,
and not faint.*

—Isaiah 40:31

Think of each problem you encounter as nothing more than a challenging reminder from God to think a little higher and reach a little farther. When met with a difficult situation along the road of life, greet it, acknowledge it, and move past it. Then you will be able to continue on your journey a little stronger, a little wiser.

Lord, you are the light I follow down this long, dark tunnel. You are the voice that whispers, urging me onward when this wall of sorrow seems insurmountable. You are the hand that reaches out and grabs mine when I feel as if I'm sinking in despair. You alone, Lord, are the waters that fill me when I am dried of all hope and faith. I thank you, Lord, for although I may feel like giving up, you have not given up on me. Amen.

As we have therefore opportunity, let us do good unto all men, especially unto them who are of the household of faith.

—Galatians 6:10

Faith is a commodity that cannot be purchased, traded, or sold. When you have faith, you have a power that can change night into day, move mountains, calm stormy seas. When you have faith, you can fall over and over again, only to get up each time more determined that ever to succeed, and you will succeed. For faith is God in action, and faith is available to anyone, rich, poor, young or old, as long as you believe.

Blessed are the peacemakers: for they shall be called the children of God.

—Matthew 5:9

Peace comes to those who know it is an inward state of mind, not an outward state of being. When we've attained inner balance and harmony, nothing that occurs outside of us can disrupt that claim. Those who have true peace of mind know that they can meet both good fortune and misfortune with a positive attitude and achieve an equally positive outcome. Inner peace depends not on outer circumstance, but on how we choose to react to it within.

The secret to happiness
lies within the present
moment. Wise is the soul
that cherishes this day, this
hour, this moment, and does
not long for other times.
Fortunate is the heart that
loves what is right in front
of it, not what it once had
or wishes it could have. And
blessed is the mind that
worries not over what was or
what might someday be, but
focuses entirely on what is.

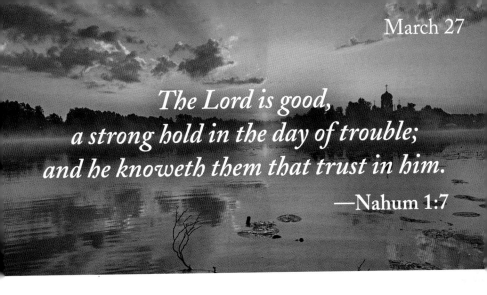

The Lord is good,
a strong hold in the day of trouble;
and he knoweth them that trust in him.

—Nahum 1:7

We have seen that inconceivable acts can cause our world to crumble around us. Yet we need not fall apart inside. If we place our trust in God's goodness, he will come to our aid and bring us comfort to restore our hope in the future. His love and compassion will lift our spirits so we can rejoice no matter what disaster or tragedy may befall us. For as long as God is beside us, nothing can defeat us or take what is truly important from us.

In my distress I called upon the Lord,
and cried unto my God:
he heard my voice out of his temple,
and my cry came before him,
even into his ears.

—Psalm 18:6

The best listeners are often silent, the depth of their understanding revealed by their actions. God is one such listener.

Nevertheless I tell you the truth; It is expedient for you that I go away: for if I go not away, the Comforter will not come unto you; but if I depart, I will send him unto you.

—John 16:7

How lonely we are when trouble strikes. Send us a sign, Lord. We long for a message, a hand reaching toward us. And just as God promised, we're visited by a presence in dream and daylight revelations, and we are grateful for God's personal, one-on-one caring.

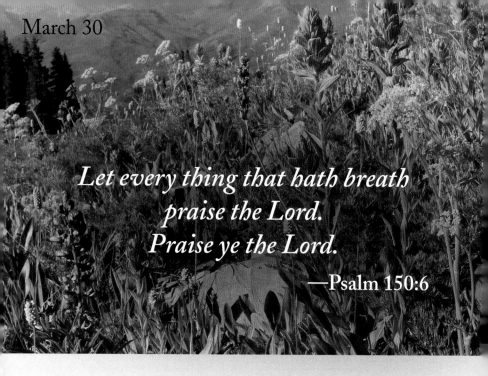

Let every thing that hath breath
praise the Lord.
Praise ye the Lord.

—Psalm 150:6

Sweet souls around us watch us still,
press nearer to our side;
into our thoughts, into our prayers,
with gentle helpings glide.
—Harriet Beecher Stowe,
"The Other World"

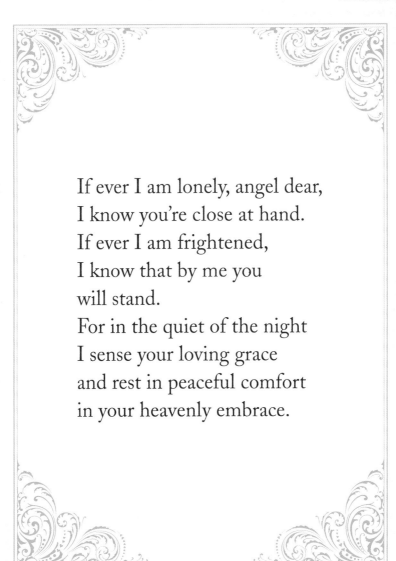

If ever I am lonely, angel dear,
I know you're close at hand.
If ever I am frightened,
I know that by me you
will stand.
For in the quiet of the night
I sense your loving grace
and rest in peaceful comfort
in your heavenly embrace.

April

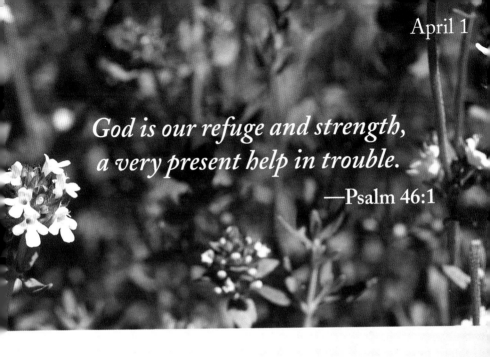

*God is our refuge and strength,
a very present help in trouble.*

—Psalm 46:1

The raging storm may round us beat,
a shelter in the time of storm;
we'll never leave our safe retreat,
a shelter in the time of storm.
Oh, Jesus is a rock in a weary land,
a weary land, a weary land;
oh, Jesus is a rock in a weary land,
a shelter in the time of storm.
—Vernon J. Charlesworth

We love him,
because he first loved us.

—1 John 4:19

Take away our bent to sinning,
Alpha and Omega be;
end of faith, as its beginning,
set our hearts at liberty.
Finish then thy new creation,
pure and spotless let us be;
let us see thy great salvation,
perfectly restored in thee.
Changed from glory into glory,
till in heaven we take our place,
till we cast our crowns before thee,
lost in wonder, love, and praise!
—Charles Wesley

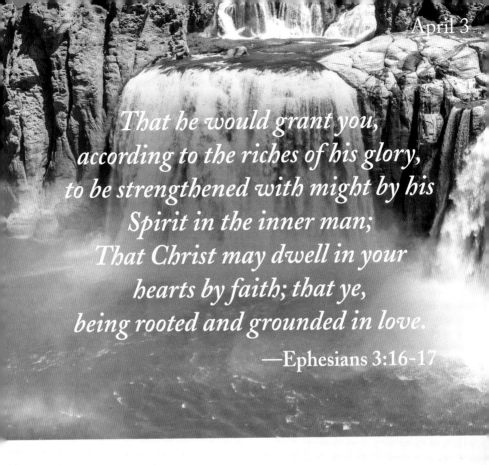

That he would grant you,
according to the riches of his glory,
to be strengthened with might by his
Spirit in the inner man;
That Christ may dwell in your
hearts by faith; that ye,
being rooted and grounded in love.

—Ephesians 3:16-17

Geese take turns, take up the slack, in the
natural rhythm of things. By sharing our
journey, we, too, gain that updraft of air,
where we'll rest awhile, knowing love is
the wind under our wings.

Whom have I in heaven but thee?
and there is none upon earth that I
desire beside thee.

—Psalm 73:25

Raise thine eyes to heaven
when thy spirits quail,
when, by tempests driven,
heart and courage fail.
All thy woe and sadness,
in this world below,
balance not the gladness
thou in heaven shalt know.
—Heinrich Siegmund Oswald, "O Let
Him Whose Sorrow"

We think of love, hope, faith and the power of prayer and forgiveness. But how often do we stop each day and give thanks for all the blessings in our lives? Are we too focused on what we lack, what we don't have, don't want, don't need? By opening the heart and mind to focus on gratitude, we unleash a treasure of unceasing good that's just waiting to overflow into our lives.

But take diligent heed to do the commandment and the law, which Moses the servant of the Lord charged you, to love the Lord your God, and to walk in all his ways, and to keep his commandments, and to cleave unto him, and to serve him with all your heart and with all your soul.

—Joshua 22:5

Hope is like the sun, which, as we journey towards it, casts the shadow of our burden behind us.
—Samuel Smiles

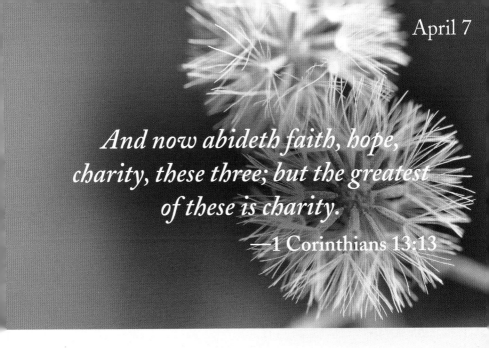

And now abideth faith, hope, charity, these three; but the greatest of these is charity.

—1 Corinthians 13:13

There is a difference between wishing that something was so and having faith that it will be. Wishing implies an attitude of hope based on fantasy and daydreams. Faith implies an attitude of belief based upon reality and intentions. You can wish for a thing all you want, but until you have complete faith that it can—and will—be yours, it will be just a wish.

*I will not leave you comfortless:
I will come to you.*

—John 14:18

Love comforteth like sunshine after rain.
—William Shakespeare

It sometimes takes a tragic event to open our eyes to the blessings that surround us, to show us the joy in life's simple moments. Day-to-day activities and events can seem mundane and repetitive until something happens that shakes our foundation and brings into sharp focus what is truly important and precious. Our family, friends, our neighbors, and our communities suddenly become havens of love, support, and comfort in the midst of tragedy.

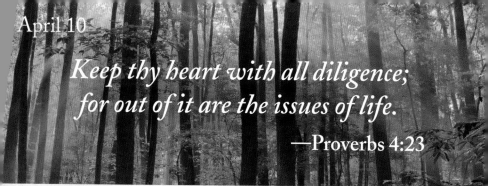

Keep thy heart with all diligence;
for out of it are the issues of life.

—Proverbs 4:23

Without suffering, there would be
no learning.
Without learning, there would be
no wisdom.
Without wisdom, there would be
no understanding.
Without understanding, there would be
no acceptance.
Without acceptance, there would be
no forgiveness.
Without forgiveness, there would be
no joy.
Without joy, there would be no love.
Without love, there would be no life.

What you have learned, teach others; what you have experienced, share with others.

Precious Lord, bless me with your grace that I may experience the deepest peace and healing only you can provide. Show me the merciful love that knows no end that I may rest today knowing I am cared for. Amen.

Why art thou cast down, O my soul?
and why art thou disquieted within
me? hope thou in God:
for I shall yet praise him,
who is the health of my countenance,
and my God.

—Psalm 42:11

No coward soul is mine
no trembler in the world's
storm-troubled sphere:
I see heaven's glories shine,
and faith shines equal,
arming me from fear.
—Emily Bronte

The law of the Lord is perfect,
converting the soul:
the testimony of the Lord is sure,
making wise the simple.

—Psalm 19:7

Lord, I believe a rest remains,
to all thy people known;
a rest where pure enjoyment reigns
and thou art loved alone;
a rest where all our soul's desire
is fixed on things above;
where fear and sin and grief expire,
cast out by perfect love.
—Charles Wesley

But the Comforter, which is the Holy Ghost, whom the Father will send in my name, he shall teach you all things, and bring all things to your remembrance, whatsoever I have said unto you.

—John 14:26

Comfort, dear God, those whose eyes are filled with tears and those whose backs are near breaking with the weight of a heavy burden. Heal those whose hearts hold a wound and whose faith has been dealt a blow. Bless all who mourn and who despair. Help those who can't imagine how they'll make it through another day. For your goodness and mercy are enough for all the troubles in the world. Amen.

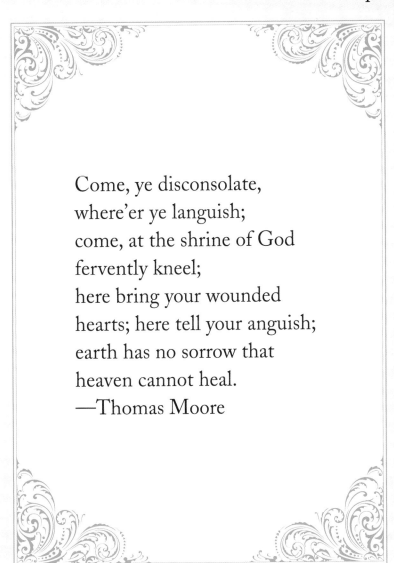

Come, ye disconsolate,
where'er ye languish;
come, at the shrine of God
fervently kneel;
here bring your wounded
hearts; here tell your anguish;
earth has no sorrow that
heaven cannot heal.
—Thomas Moore

The heavens declare the glory of God; and the firmament sheweth his handywork. Day unto day uttereth speech, and night unto night sheweth knowledge.

—Psalm 19:1-2

Like sun that melts the snow,
my soul absorbs the grace
that beats in gentle, healing rays
from some godly place.
Like rain that heals parched earth,
my body drinks the love
that falls in gently, soothing waves
from heaven up above.

Train up a child in the way he should go:
and when he is old, he will not depart from it.

—Proverbs 22:6

Heavenly Father, when I was young, I thought all things hurt or broken could be fixed: knees, feelings, bicycles, tea sets. Now I've learned that not everything can be repaired, relived, or cured. As a mother comforts her child, heal my hurting and grant me the peace I used to know. This I pray. Amen.

God, I give thanks for the
wisdom you share with
me when I am trying to
understand my own actions
or someone else's. You know
what is best, and you have my
highest good in mind. I will
turn to you for the advice and
guidance I need. Thank you,
God, for being a strong and
loving presence in my life.
Amen.

But the fruit of the spirit is love, joy, peace, longsuffering, gentleness, goodness, faith, Meekness, temperance: against such there is no law.

—Galatians 5:22-23

God, grant me the courage to let go of shame, guilt, and anger. Free me of all negative energies, for only then will I become a conduit for joy and a channel for goodness. Amen.

Lord, I need you to help me with the concept of forgiving people over and over again for the same behavior. I know you taught that there was no limit to the number of times we should forgive someone, but I get so weary of doing it, Lord. Help me to have a heart of forgiveness, so ready to forgive that I do so before the person who has wronged me even seeks my forgiveness. There's freedom in that kind of forgiveness, Lord. Help me claim it for my own. Amen.

*He that getteth wisdom loveth
his own soul:
he that keepeth understanding
shall find good.*

—Proverbs 19:8

Lord, help me understand that the
challenges I am going through serve to
empower me. Teach me the wisdom to
discern that my trials mold me into
something far grander than even I could
have imagined. Amen.

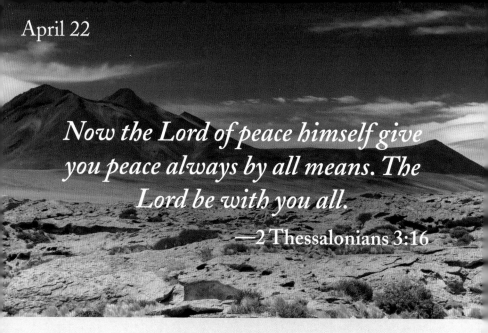

Now the Lord of peace himself give you peace always by all means. The Lord be with you all.

—2 Thessalonians 3:16

Comfort me in my day of need with a love that is infinite and true. Ignore my lack of desire to forgive and forget. Fill my anger with the waters of peace and serenity that I may come to accept this situation and move on to a greater level of understanding and knowing.

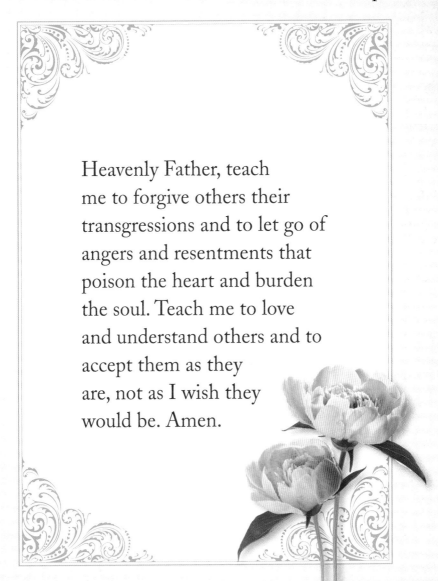

Heavenly Father, teach
me to forgive others their
transgressions and to let go of
angers and resentments that
poison the heart and burden
the soul. Teach me to love
and understand others and to
accept them as they
are, not as I wish they
would be. Amen.

*Whom having not seen, ye love;
in whom, though now ye see him
not, yet believing, ye rejoice with
joy unspeakable and full of glory:
Receiving the end of your faith,
even the salvation of your souls.*

—1 Peter 1:8-9

Faith in a wise and trustworthy God, even
in broken times like these, teaches us a
new math: subtracting old ways and
adding new thoughts because sharing
with God divides our troubles and
multiplies unfathomable possibilities
for renewed life.

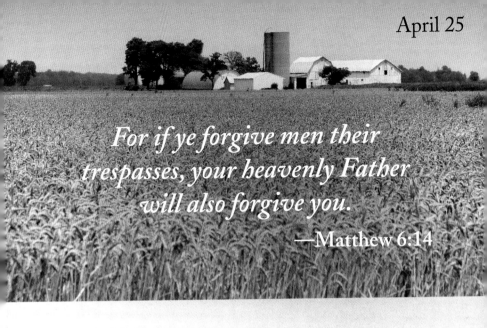

For if ye forgive men their trespasses, your heavenly Father will also forgive you.

—Matthew 6:14

Lord, your forgiveness, based on your love for me, has transformed my life. I've experienced inner healing and freedom in knowing that you have wiped my slate clean and made me your friend. Help me to become an extension of your love to those around me. Let healing happen as I apply the salve to the wounds they inflict on me. Please strengthen me while I carry it out in your name. Amen.

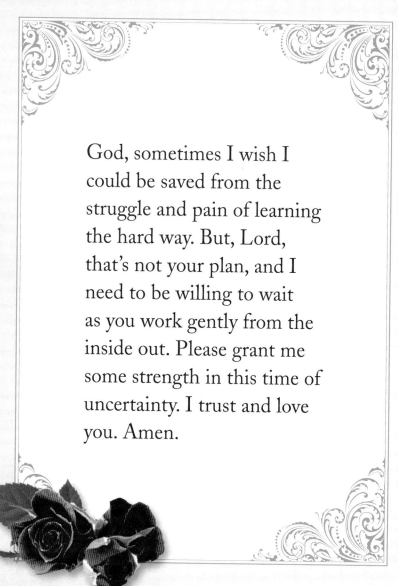

God, sometimes I wish I could be saved from the struggle and pain of learning the hard way. But, Lord, that's not your plan, and I need to be willing to wait as you work gently from the inside out. Please grant me some strength in this time of uncertainty. I trust and love you. Amen.

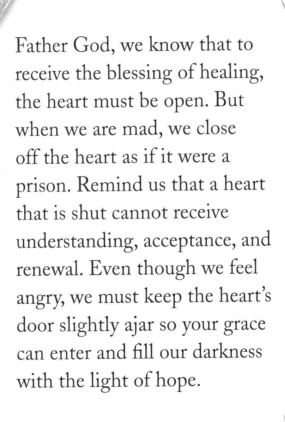

Father God, we know that to receive the blessing of healing, the heart must be open. But when we are mad, we close off the heart as if it were a prison. Remind us that a heart that is shut cannot receive understanding, acceptance, and renewal. Even though we feel angry, we must keep the heart's door slightly ajar so your grace can enter and fill our darkness with the light of hope.

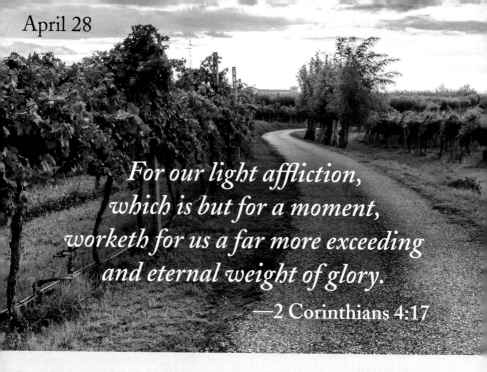

*For our light affliction,
which is but for a moment,
worketh for us a far more exceeding
and eternal weight of glory.*
—2 Corinthians 4:17

I know you will not fail to lift me up from
my sorrow and gently deposit me upon the
shore. And though my body is tired and
my spirit is weary from weeping, I offer
myself to you in complete surrender, so
that you may fill my nets with the bounty
of your eternal peace and the comfort of
your infinite love.

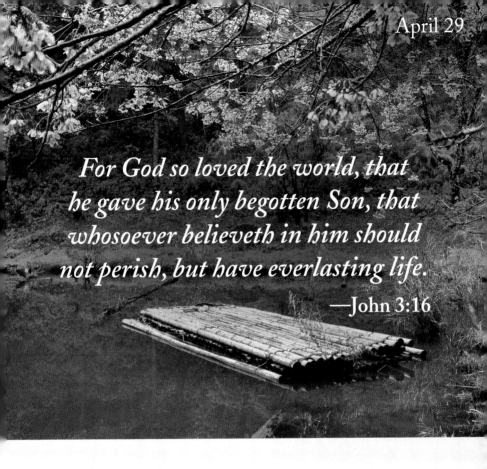

For God so loved the world, that he gave his only begotten Son, that whosoever believeth in him should not perish, but have everlasting life.

—John 3:16

God, thank you for letting me cling to the faith that has sustained me through so much uncertainty and pain before. I now know that although faith may be all I have, it's also all I need.

Let us meditate upon the Lord's holy name, that we may trust him the better and rejoice the more readily. He is in character holy, just, true, gracious, faithful and unchanging. Is not such a God to be trusted? He is allwise, almighty, and everywhere present; can we not cheerfully rely on him?... They that know thy name will trust thee; and they that trust thee will rejoice in thee, O Lord.

—Charles Spurgeon

May

Though I speak with the tongues of men and of angels, and have not charity, I am become as sounding brass, or a tinkling cymbal.

—1 Corinthians 13:1

Let each new blossom peeking out at the sun remind you of angels luxuriating in heaven's light. Then lay your head back, feel that same sun on your face, count your blessings, and enjoy the luxury the angels do.

Almighty God, sometimes the floods of life leave us devastated and defeated. Our tears flow like rivers pushing over their banks. In our worst moments, you give us comfort and hope.

When the quiet after the storm finally comes to our hearts, we look up to find that God is still with us, holding us close to his heart.

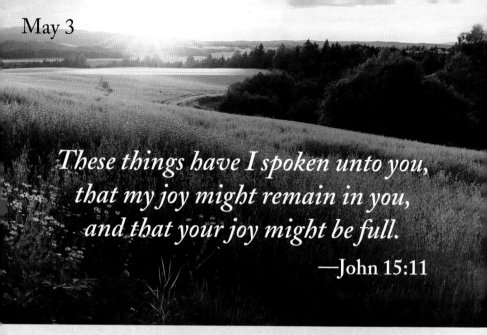

These things have I spoken unto you, that my joy might remain in you, and that your joy might be full.

—John 15:11

Doing nothing for others is the undoing of one's self. We must be purposely kind and generous, or we miss the best part of existence. The heart that goes out of itself gets large and full of joy. This is the great secret of inner life. We do ourselves the most good when we are doing something for others.

—Horace Mann

*But thou, O man of God, flee
these things; and follow after
righteousness, godliness, faith, love,
patience, meekness.*

—1 Timothy 6:11

Love is faith, and faith, like a gathered
flower, will live rootlessly on.
—Thomas Hardy

Give to the winds thy fears
hope and be undismayed;
God hears thy sighs and
counts thy tears God shall lift
up thy head. Through waves
and clouds and storms, he
gently clears thy way.
Wait thou his time; so shall
this night soon end in joyous
day. Let us in life, death,
they steadfast truth declare
and publish with our
latest breath thy love and
guardian care.
—Paul Gerhardt,
        translated by John Wesley

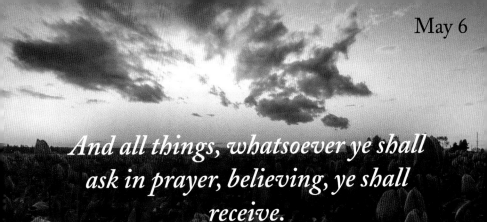

And all things, whatsoever ye shall ask in prayer, believing, ye shall receive.

—Matthew 21:22

Knowledge stops at the edge of the earth. Faith goes beyond the stars, illimitable, calm, all-comprehending. The wisdom of the world is a surface wisdom and breeds only a surface humor. The wisdom of faith reaches from heaven to hell, into the heart of all living; and when it smiles the angels of God smile with it.
—Reverend F. X. Lasance

O most blessed light Divine,
shine within these hearts of
thine, and our inmost
being fill:
Where thou art not, man
hath nought,
nothing good in deed or
thought, nothing free from
taint of ill.

—Whitsuntide, Book of
Common Prayer,
Church of England

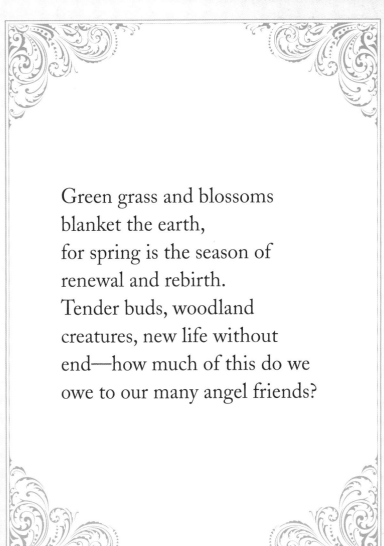

Green grass and blossoms
blanket the earth,
for spring is the season of
renewal and rebirth.
Tender buds, woodland
creatures, new life without
end—how much of this do we
owe to our many angel friends?

Confusion is directing my thoughts. My mind loyally follows its erratic demands and becomes increasingly lost and frustrated. I need a sign to orient myself and to find my way out of this turmoil. Find me, Lord, for I am wandering in the wilderness of my own mind, heading deeper and deeper into despair. Where are you? I call. And then I realize that by describing my lostness, you show me where I am and how to return home.

But sanctify the Lord God in your hearts: and be ready always to give an answer to every man that asketh you a reason of the hope that is in you with meekness and fear.

—1 Peter 3:15

Hope is the lone flower blooming in times of life's desert.

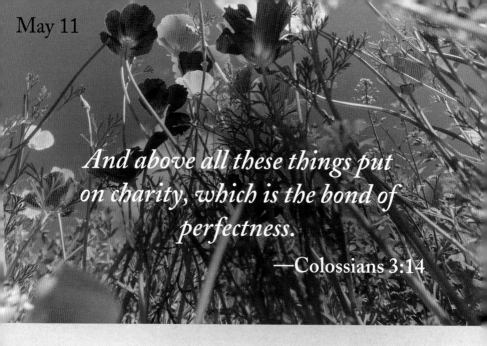

And above all these things put on charity, which is the bond of perfectness.

—Colossians 3:14

The sunshine of your caring gaze,
the water of your gentle words,
the nourishment of your tender touch
have revived this limp flower called my
soul. I am once again in full bloom
because of your love.

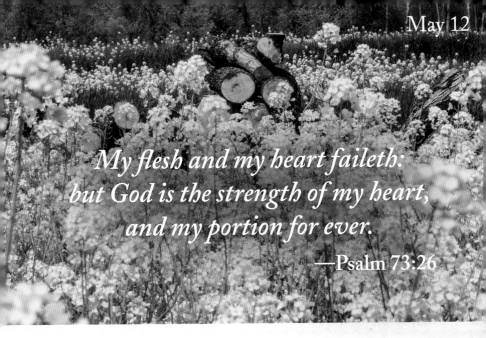

My flesh and my heart faileth:
but God is the strength of my heart,
and my portion for ever.

—Psalm 73:26

Each new stage draws me like a bee to flower. There, hope prompts me to unfold the petals and dine on the nectar of my future.

The best things are nearest:
breath in your nostrils, light in
your eyes, flowers at your feet,
duties at your hand, the path
of God just before you.
—Robert Louis Stevenson

Dear Father God, you sent
your son to us to be our Lord,
to watch over us, to bring us
comfort, strength, hope, and
healing when our hearts are
broken and our lives seem
shattered. We will never be
alone, not when you are here
with us always and
forever. Remind us
to look to you
for strength.
Amen.

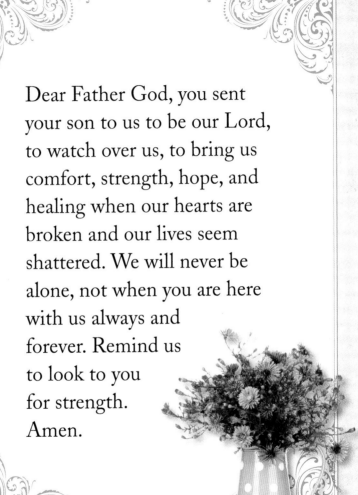

He is thy gracious friend
and (O my Soul awake!)
Did in pure love descend,
to die here for thy sake.
If thou canst get but thither,
There grows
the flow'r of peace,
the rose that cannot wither,
thy fortress, and thy ease.
leave then thy foolish ranges,
for none can thee secure,
but One, who never changes,
thy God, thy life, thy cure.
—Henry Vaughan

For he that will love life, and see good days, let him refrain his tongue from evil, and his lips that they speak no guile: Let him eschew evil, and do good; let him seek peace, and ensue it.

—1 Peter 3:10-11

Our worries are hard to dismiss, Lord. They seem to grow bigger and bigger until they take over our lives. Please help us conquer them, one at a time. Your reassurance is welcome. Amen.

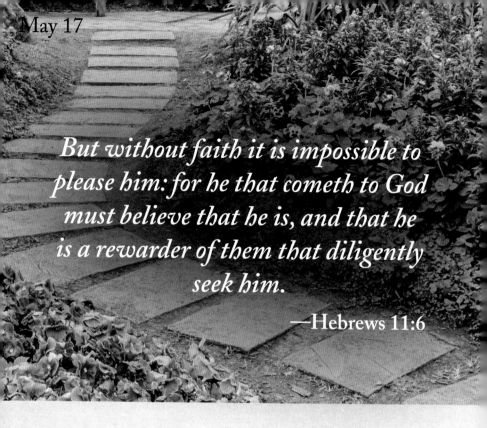

But without faith it is impossible to please him: for he that cometh to God must believe that he is, and that he is a rewarder of them that diligently seek him.

—Hebrews 11:6

Faith is the foundation upon which a happy, healthy life is built. The stronger our faith, the less our life can be shaken by outside occurrences and extraneous circumstances.

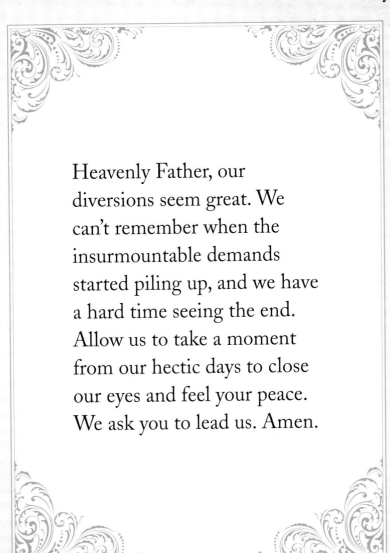

Heavenly Father, our diversions seem great. We can't remember when the insurmountable demands started piling up, and we have a hard time seeing the end. Allow us to take a moment from our hectic days to close our eyes and feel your peace. We ask you to lead us. Amen.

Mental illness can be so devastating, Lord.

Few understand the heartaches involved in diseases that carry no apparent physical scars. Be with those friends, neighbors, and family members who deal daily with difficult situations of which we are often unaware. Touch them with your special love, and let them know that they can lean on you, Lord. Ease their burdens, quell their sadness, and calm their desperation. Bring peace and healing to these households.

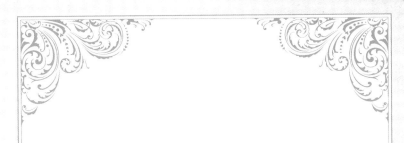

Sometimes I feel abandoned, Lord. I feel empty inside, and it's hard to connect with myself, with others, and with the world. I almost lose faith at these times, Lord. Please stay with me and help me remember your love, your light, and your peace.

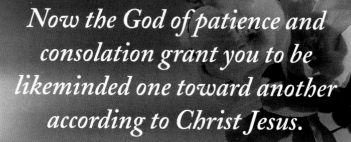

Now the God of patience and consolation grant you to be likeminded one toward another according to Christ Jesus.

—Romans 15:5

Dear God, please send your peace to calm us when we're overwhelmed. Your presence wipes away depression and despair. It renews our hope and lifts our hearts. Amen.

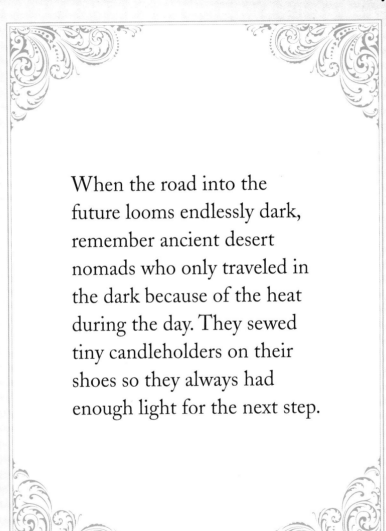

When the road into the future looms endlessly dark, remember ancient desert nomads who only traveled in the dark because of the heat during the day. They sewed tiny candleholders on their shoes so they always had enough light for the next step.

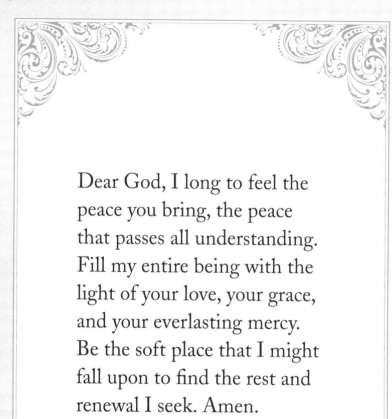

Dear God, I long to feel the
peace you bring, the peace
that passes all understanding.
Fill my entire being with the
light of your love, your grace,
and your everlasting mercy.
Be the soft place that I might
fall upon to find the rest and
renewal I seek. Amen.

When we struggle in unfamiliar territory, Lord, we feel your calming, guiding hand and remember that you have always been faithful to your children. Then we know that our journey is safe. Please continue to give us confidence as we move to where you are calling us.

In the aftermath of tragedy, it takes energy and courage to rebuild, Great Architect. How amazing that your gift of courage translates worry into energy and fear into determination. Help us recognize ill feelings as potential fuel that can be turned into reconstruction tools. Through your grace, we've courageously faced what was our lives and we are now off to see what our lives can be.

Blessed Creator, I long to feel
a sense of unity and harmony
with all that you have
created. Help me understand
that natural disasters are
opportunities for renewal
and that around every storm
cloud, a silver lining waits for
the one who has faith in you.
Let it be.

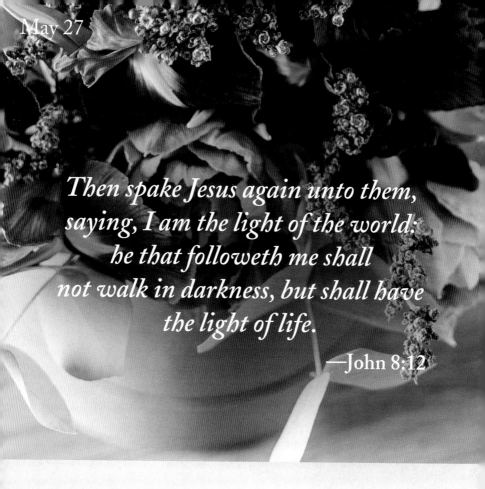

Then spake Jesus again unto them, saying, I am the light of the world: he that followeth me shall not walk in darkness, but shall have the light of life.

—John 8:12

A single sunbeam is enough to drive away many shadows.
—Saint Francis of Assisi

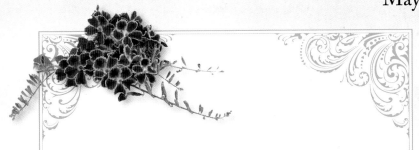

God, you are invisible but not
unseen. You reveal yourself
in creation and demonstrate
your kindness in a stranger's
sincere smile. You are
intangible but not unfelt. You
caress our faces with the wind
and embrace us in a friend's
arms. We look for you and
feel your presence. Amen.

Grace of my heart, I turn to you when I am feeling lost and alone. You restore me with strength and hope and the courage to face a new day. You bless me with joy and comfort me through trials and tribulations. You direct my thoughts, guide my actions, and temper my words. You give me the patience and kindness I need to be good. Grace of my heart, I turn to you. Amen.

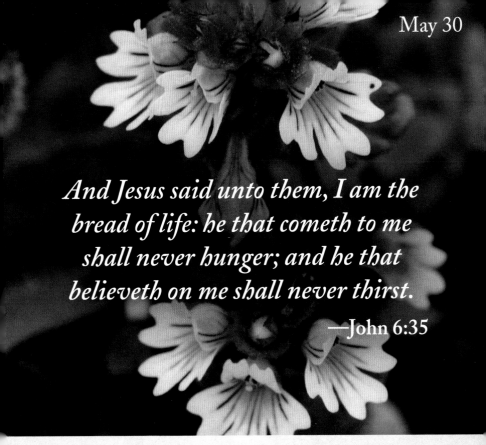

And Jesus said unto them, I am the bread of life: he that cometh to me shall never hunger; and he that believeth on me shall never thirst.

—John 6:35

Heavenly Father, your grace can refresh and renew us with the living water of hope and faith. Please help us fully live the lives you have given us. Amen.

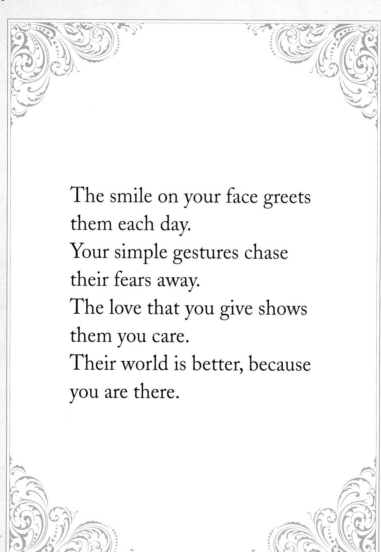

The smile on your face greets
them each day.
Your simple gestures chase
their fears away.
The love that you give shows
them you care.
Their world is better, because
you are there.

June

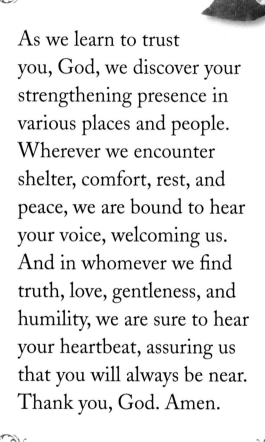

As we learn to trust
you, God, we discover your
strengthening presence in
various places and people.
Wherever we encounter
shelter, comfort, rest, and
peace, we are bound to hear
your voice, welcoming us.
And in whomever we find
truth, love, gentleness, and
humility, we are sure to hear
your heartbeat, assuring us
that you will always be near.
Thank you, God. Amen.

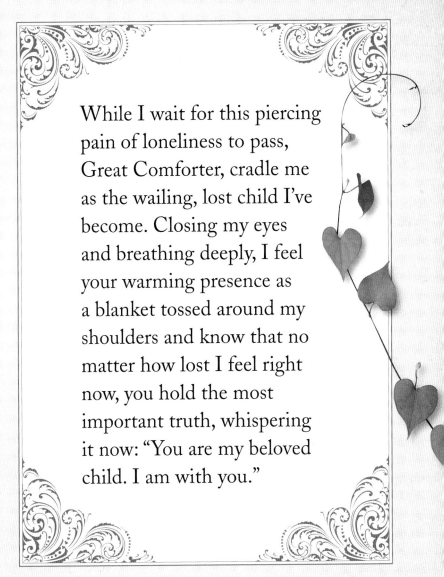

While I wait for this piercing pain of loneliness to pass, Great Comforter, cradle me as the wailing, lost child I've become. Closing my eyes and breathing deeply, I feel your warming presence as a blanket tossed around my shoulders and know that no matter how lost I feel right now, you hold the most important truth, whispering it now: "You are my beloved child. I am with you."

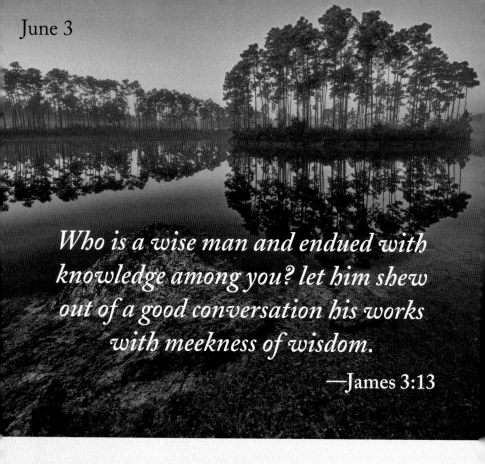

Who is a wise man and endued with knowledge among you? let him shew out of a good conversation his works with meekness of wisdom.

—James 3:13

As spring turns into summer, I thank God for granting me friends with whom to share nature's bounty.

Child, even this day, trust!
And tomorrow have faith,
and on all tomorrows! The
darkness grow less. Trust!
And each day when first
gleams the dawn-breath,
awake thou to pray; God is
wakeful to bless!
—Victor Hugo, "Trust in
God"

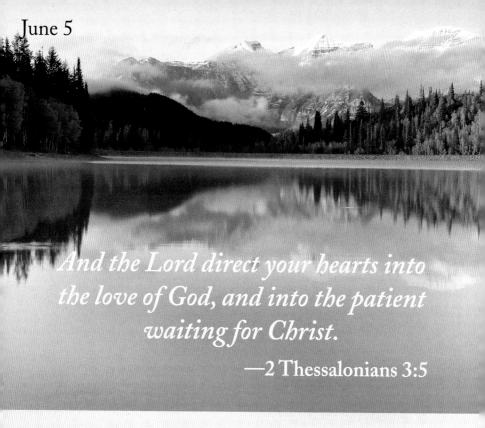

And the Lord direct your hearts into the love of God, and into the patient waiting for Christ.

—2 Thessalonians 3:5

God of all comfort, I know that with you by my side I am never alone. Your perfect love casts out all fear, doubt, and uncertainty. Your presence emboldens and empowers me. You are the light that leads me to safety again. Amen.

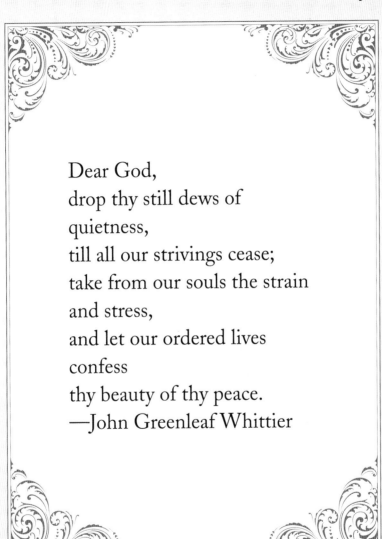

Dear God,
drop thy still dews of
quietness,
till all our strivings cease;
take from our souls the strain
and stress,
and let our ordered lives
confess
thy beauty of thy peace.
—John Greenleaf Whittier

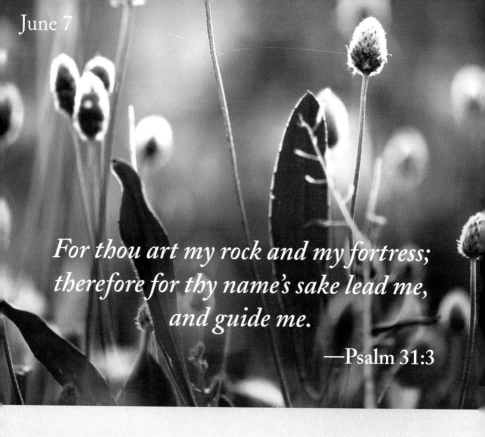

*For thou art my rock and my fortress;
therefore for thy name's sake lead me,
and guide me.*

—Psalm 31:3

Lord, please be my strength. When I am
scared, please make me brave. When I am
unsteady, please bring your stability to me.
I look to your power for an escape from
the pain. I welcome your comfort. Amen.

Beloved, now are we the sons of God, and it doth not yet appear what we shall be: but we know that, when he shall appear, we shall be like him; for we shall see him as he is. And every man that hath this hope in him purifieth himself, even as he is pure.

—1 John 3:2-3

O may thy spirit guide my feet
in ways of righteousness;
make every path of duty straight,
and plain before my face. Amen.

But as it is written, Eye hath not seen, nor ear heard, neither have entered into the heart of man, the things which God hath prepared for them that love him.

—1 Corinthians 2:9

His love is wider than our worries, longer than our loneliness, stronger than our sorrows, deeper than our doubts, and higher than our hostilities. This is why valleys are so wide, rivers so long, winds so strong, oceans so deep, and the sky is so high—with these, we can have a picture of the wonder of his love.

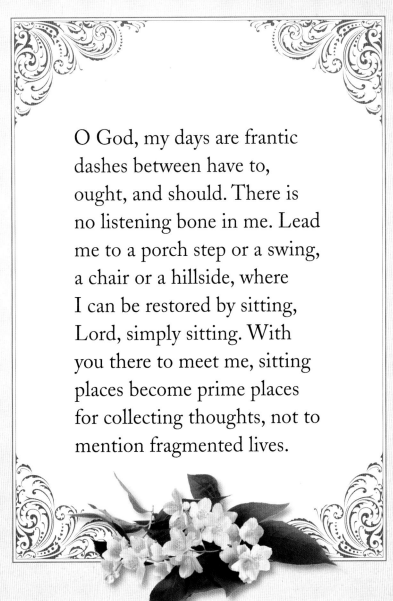

O God, my days are frantic
dashes between have to,
ought, and should. There is
no listening bone in me. Lead
me to a porch step or a swing,
a chair or a hillside, where
I can be restored by sitting,
Lord, simply sitting. With
you there to meet me, sitting
places become prime places
for collecting thoughts, not to
mention fragmented lives.

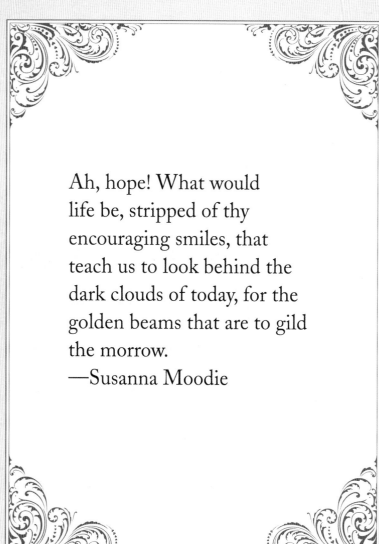

Ah, hope! What would life be, stripped of thy encouraging smiles, that teach us to look behind the dark clouds of today, for the golden beams that are to gild the morrow.
—Susanna Moodie

And thou shalt love the Lord thy God with all thy heart, and with all thy soul, and with all thy mind, and with all thy strength: this is the first commandment.

—Mark 12:30

Here is a place you can stop and rest for a while. Here is a place you can lay down your worries and let go of the weight of your fears upon your shoulders. Here is a place you can breathe deeply of fresh air, and feel the warmth of the sun on your skin. Here is a place filled with tranquility, like a beautiful garden. Here is where you are, with God.

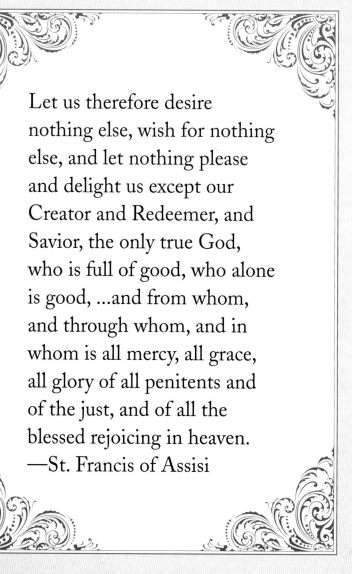

Let us therefore desire
nothing else, wish for nothing
else, and let nothing please
and delight us except our
Creator and Redeemer, and
Savior, the only true God,
who is full of good, who alone
is good, ...and from whom,
and through whom, and in
whom is all mercy, all grace,
all glory of all penitents and
of the just, and of all the
blessed rejoicing in heaven.
—St. Francis of Assisi

A new commandment I give unto you, That ye love one another; as I have loved you, that ye also love one another.

—John 13:34

When my way is drear, Precious Lord,
linger near.
When the day is almost gone,
hear my cry, hear my call,
hold my hand, lest I fall,
Precious Lord, take my hand,
lead me home.

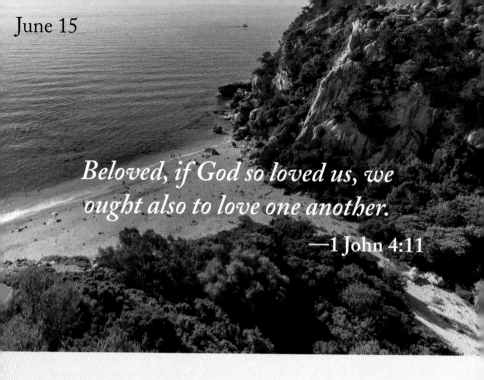

Beloved, if God so loved us, we ought also to love one another.

—1 John 4:11

When trouble strikes, O God, we are restored by small signs of hope found in ordinary places: friends, random kindness, shared pain and support. Help us collect them like mustard seeds that can grow into a spreading harvest of well-being.

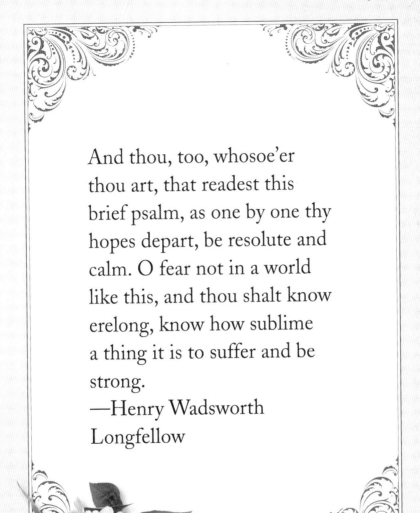

And thou, too, whosoe'er
thou art, that readest this
brief psalm, as one by one thy
hopes depart, be resolute and
calm. O fear not in a world
like this, and thou shalt know
erelong, know how sublime
a thing it is to suffer and be
strong.
—Henry Wadsworth
Longfellow

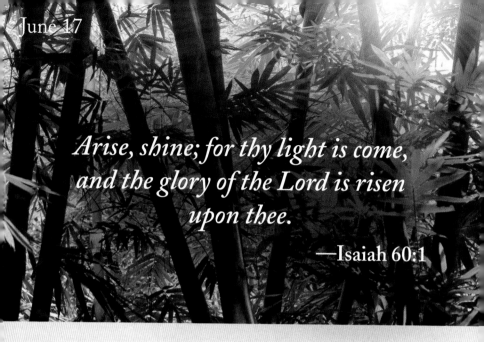

Arise, shine; for thy light is come, and the glory of the Lord is risen upon thee.

—Isaiah 60:1

Like the gentle flicker of a candle burning
in the darkness,
hope overcomes all.
Like a soft breeze that cools the body on a
hot summer day,
hope refreshes all.
Like the song of birds announcing
morning after a lonely night,
hope comforts all.

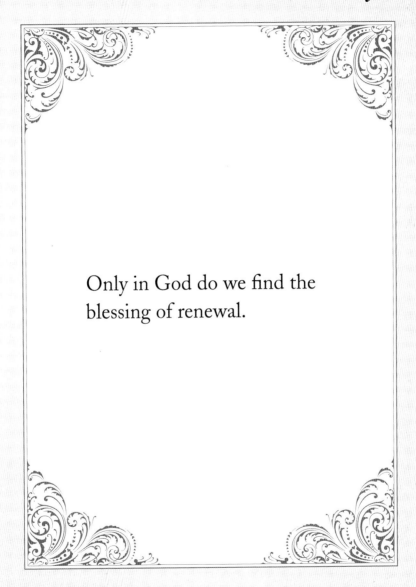

Only in God do we find the
blessing of renewal.

Rejoiceth not in iniquity, but rejoiceth in the truth; Beareth all things, believeth all things, hopeth all things, endureth all things.

—1 Corinthians 13:6-7

Renounce all strength, but strength divine,
And peace shall be for ever thine.
—William Cowper

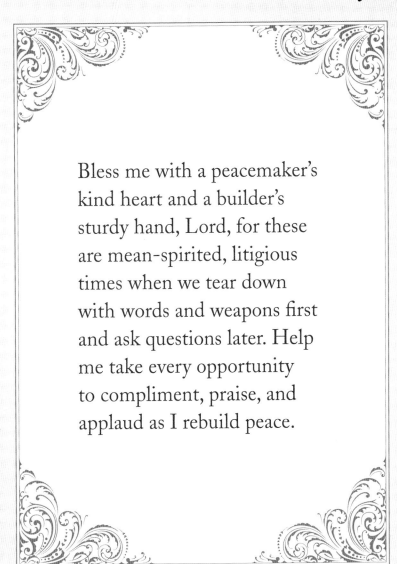

Bless me with a peacemaker's kind heart and a builder's sturdy hand, Lord, for these are mean-spirited, litigious times when we tear down with words and weapons first and ask questions later. Help me take every opportunity to compliment, praise, and applaud as I rebuild peace.

Commit thy way unto the Lord;
trust also in him; and he shall bring
it to pass.
And he shall bring forth thy
righteousness as the light,
and thy judgment as the noonday.

—Psalm 37:5-6

For it is only the finite that has wrought
and suffered; the infinite lies stretched in
smiling repose.
—Ralph Waldo Emerson

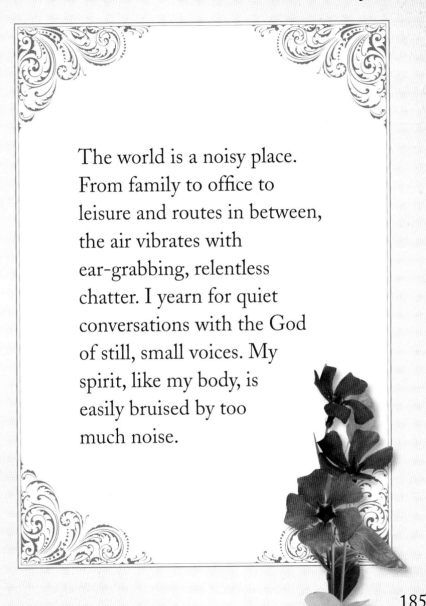

The world is a noisy place. From family to office to leisure and routes in between, the air vibrates with ear-grabbing, relentless chatter. I yearn for quiet conversations with the God of still, small voices. My spirit, like my body, is easily bruised by too much noise.

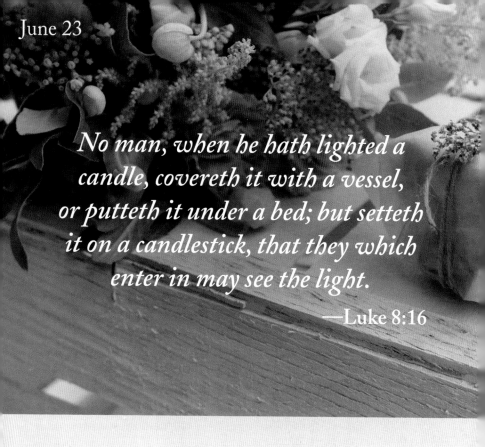

*No man, when he hath lighted a
candle, covereth it with a vessel,
or putteth it under a bed; but setteth
it on a candlestick, that they which
enter in may see the light.*

—Luke 8:16

Teach me to feel another's woe,
to hide the fault I see;
that mercy I to others show,
that mercy show to me.
—Alexander Pope

*The statutes of the Lord are right,
rejoicing the heart:
the commandment of the Lord is pure,
enlightening the eyes.*

—Psalm 19:8

Never let our need overshadow our
recognition of the needs of others. Ground
us in empathy. Commission our sympathy.
Urge us to offer comforting hands and
understanding hearts. And in so doing,
show us how easing the pain of others
eases our own.

*The Lord will give
strength unto his people;
the Lord will bless
his people with peace.*

—Psalm 29:11

Hope springs eternal in the human breast:
man never is, but always to be, blest.
The soul, uneasy and confin'd from home
rests and expatiates in a life to come.
—Alexander Pope

Though long the weary way
we tread,
and sorrow crown each
lingering year,
no path we shun, no darkness
dead,
our hearts still whispering,
thou art near!
—Oliver Wendell Holmes

*I will both lay me down in peace,
and sleep: for thou, Lord,
only makest me dwell in safety.*

—Psalm 4:8

Lord, make me an instrument of your
peace, where there is hatred, let me sow
love; where there is injury, pardon; where
there is doubt, faith...
—St. Francis of Assisi

Finally, brethren, farewell.
Be perfect, be of good comfort,
be of one mind, live in peace;
and the God of love and peace shall
be with you.

—2 Corinthians 13:11

Blessings on him who invented sleep, the cloak that covers all human thoughts, the food that satisfies hunger, the drink that quenches thirst...
—Miguel de Cervantes

When we observe the last
morning glory stretching
faithfully to receive what
warmth is left in the chilly
sunshine, we are heartened
and inspired to do the same.
When we are hesitant to
speak up and then read in the
newspaper a story of courage
and controversy, we find our
voice lifted and strengthened
by your message in black-
and-white type. Lord, we
are grateful receivers of all
the angelic messages that
surround us every day.

Though like the wanderer,
the sun gone down,
darkness be over me,
my rest a stone;
yet in my dreams I'd be
nearer, my God, to thee,
nearer to thee!
...Then, with my waking
thoughts
bright with thy praise,
out of my stony griefs,
bethel I'll raise;
So by my woes to be
nearer, my God, to thee,
nearer to thee!
—Sarah Flower Adams,
    "Nearer to Thee"

July

Raise thine eyes to heaven
when thy spirits quail,
when, by tempests driven,
heart and courage fail.
When in grief we languish,
he will dry the tear,
who his children's anguish
soothes with succour near.
All our woe and sadness,
in this world below,
balance not the gladness,
we in heaven shall know.
—General Hymn #286,
     Book of Common Prayer

For the mountains shall depart,
and the hills be removed;
but my kindness shall not depart
from thee,
neither shall the covenant of my
peace be removed,
saith the Lord that hath mercy
on thee.

—Isaiah 54:10

There is no hope unmingled with fear, and
no fear unmingled with hope.
—Baruch de Spinoza

Be patient with everyone, but above all with yourself...do not be disheartened by your imperfections, but always rise up with fresh courage. How are we to be patient in dealing with our neighbor's faults if we are impatient in dealing with our own?
—Saint Francis de Sales

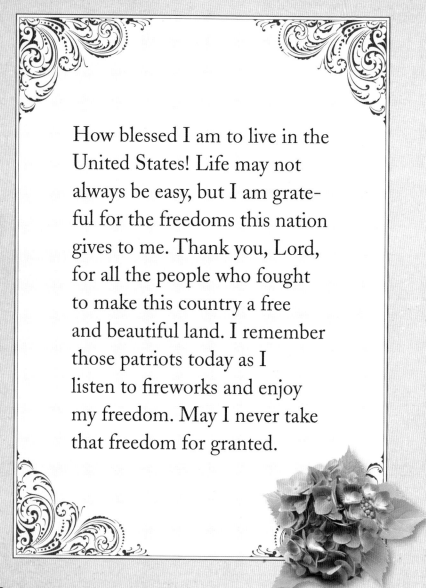

How blessed I am to live in the
United States! Life may not
always be easy, but I am grateful for the freedoms this nation
gives to me. Thank you, Lord,
for all the people who fought
to make this country a free
and beautiful land. I remember
those patriots today as I
listen to fireworks and enjoy
my freedom. May I never take
that freedom for granted.

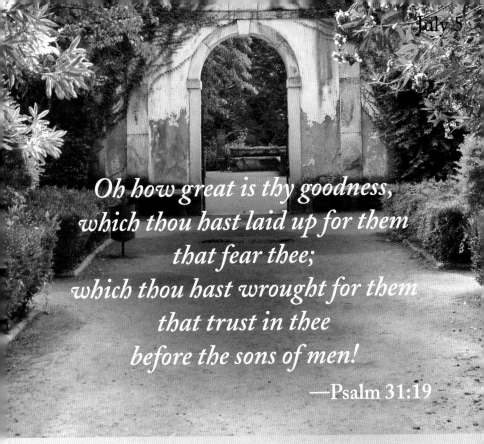

Oh how great is thy goodness,
which thou hast laid up for them
that fear thee;
which thou hast wrought for them
that trust in thee
before the sons of men!

—Psalm 31:19

I'm not afraid of storms, for I'm learning
how to sail my ship.
—Louisa May Alcott

May you be assured of God's presence as you weather this storm. As the waves toss you about, and the ship of your life threatens to crash into rough rocks: He is there. Never despair. For no wind or water, rock or sand has the power to defeat his plans for you. And, after all, he created all these things, and in him alone they have their existence.

And it shall come to pass, if thou shalt hearken diligently unto the voice of the Lord thy God, to observe and to do all his commandments which I command thee this day, that the Lord thy God will set thee on high above all nations of the earth.

—Deuteronomy 28:1

All is a miracle. The stupendous order of nature, the revolution of a hundred millions of worlds around a million of stars, the activity of light, the life of all animals, all are grand and perpetual miracles.
—Voltaire

As above the darkest
storm cloud
shines the sun, serenely bright
waiting to restore to nature
all the glory of his light,
so, behind each cloud
of sorrow,
so, in each affliction, stands,
hid, an angel, with a blessing
from the Father in his hand.
—Daniel H. Howard

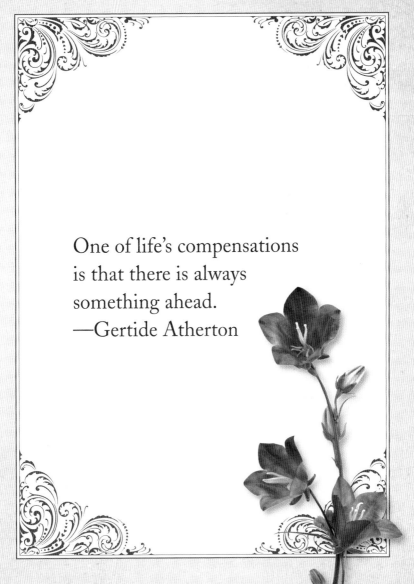

One of life's compensations
is that there is always
something ahead.
—Gertide Atherton

But the wisdom that is from above is first pure, then peaceable, gentle, and easy to be intreated, full of mercy and good fruits, without partiality, and without hypocrisy.

—James 3:17

We don't receive wisdom; we must discover it for ourselves after a journey that no one can take for us or spare us.
—Marcel Proust

*His lord said unto him, Well done,
thou good and faithful servant:
thou hast been faithful over a few
things, I will make thee ruler
over many things: enter thou into
the joy of thy lord.*

—Matthew 25:21

A joy that's shared is a joy made double.
—English Proverb

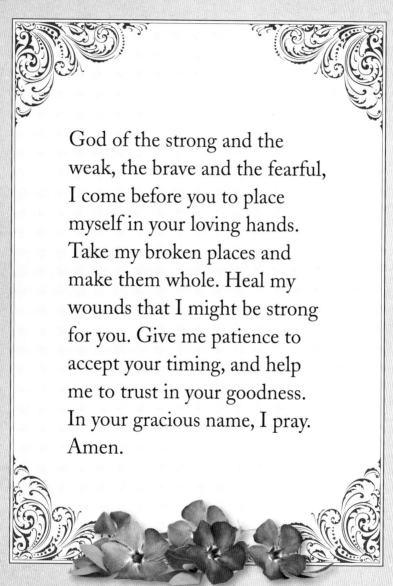

God of the strong and the weak, the brave and the fearful, I come before you to place myself in your loving hands. Take my broken places and make them whole. Heal my wounds that I might be strong for you. Give me patience to accept your timing, and help me to trust in your goodness. In your gracious name, I pray. Amen.

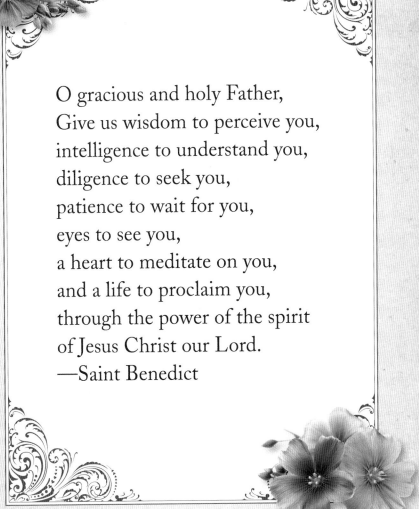

O gracious and holy Father,
Give us wisdom to perceive you,
intelligence to understand you,
diligence to seek you,
patience to wait for you,
eyes to see you,
a heart to meditate on you,
and a life to proclaim you,
through the power of the spirit
of Jesus Christ our Lord.
—Saint Benedict

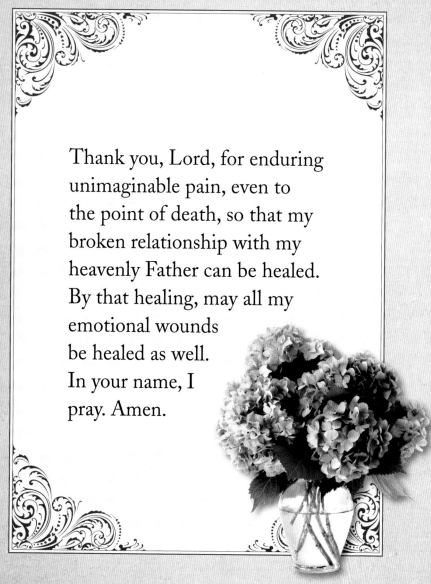

Thank you, Lord, for enduring
unimaginable pain, even to
the point of death, so that my
broken relationship with my
heavenly Father can be healed.
By that healing, may all my
emotional wounds
be healed as well.
In your name, I
pray. Amen.

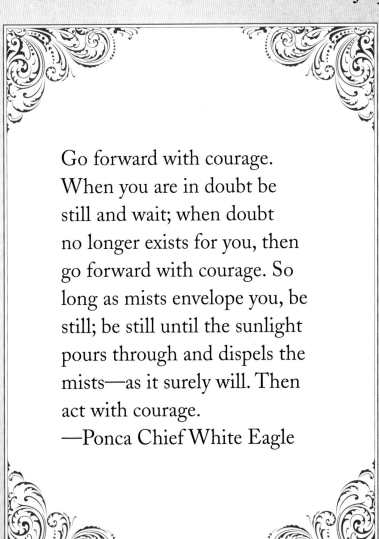

Go forward with courage.
When you are in doubt be
still and wait; when doubt
no longer exists for you, then
go forward with courage. So
long as mists envelope you, be
still; be still until the sunlight
pours through and dispels the
mists—as it surely will. Then
act with courage.
—Ponca Chief White Eagle

Gracious and healing God,
Thank you for everything you
have done for me in the past.
You have restored me in
unexpected ways and I will
never be the same.

Thank you for being with
me in the present and for the
bright future you have planned
for me. I pray for those who
don't know you yet, who don't
understand how you bless them
again and again.

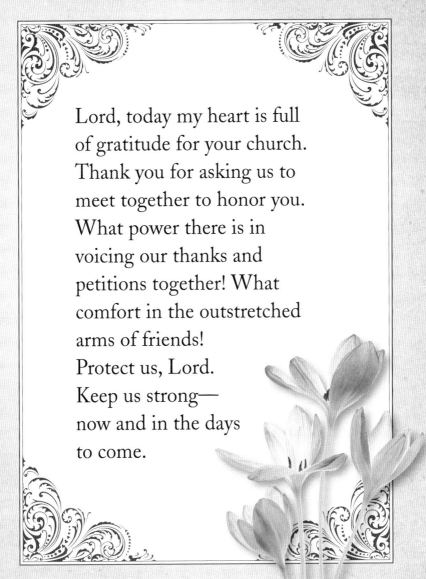

Lord, today my heart is full
of gratitude for your church.
Thank you for asking us to
meet together to honor you.
What power there is in
voicing our thanks and
petitions together! What
comfort in the outstretched
arms of friends!
Protect us, Lord.
Keep us strong—
now and in the days
to come.

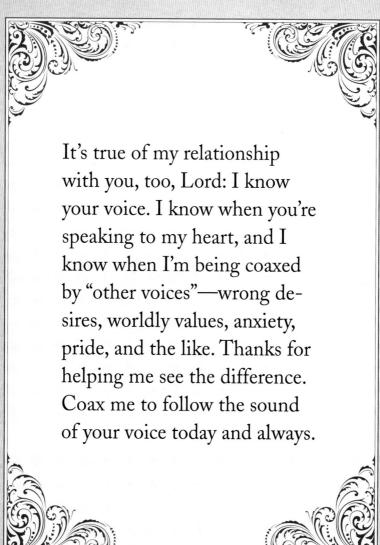

It's true of my relationship
with you, too, Lord: I know
your voice. I know when you're
speaking to my heart, and I
know when I'm being coaxed
by "other voices"—wrong desires, worldly values, anxiety,
pride, and the like. Thanks for
helping me see the difference.
Coax me to follow the sound
of your voice today and always.

Say not thou, What is the cause that the former days were better than these? for thou dost not enquire wisely concerning this.

—Ecclesiastes 7:10

Lord, today I ask your special blessing on the elderly among us. No matter how old we are, we notice our bodies aging. How difficult it must be to be near the end of life and struggling to hold on to mobility, vision, hearing, and wellness of being. Give us compassion for those older than we are, Lord, and thank you for your promise that you will be with us to the very end of our days.

Be strong and of a good courage,
fear not, nor be afraid of them:
for the Lord thy God,
he it is that doth go with thee;
he will not fail thee, nor forsake thee.

—Deuteronomy 31:6

It takes moral courage to grieve. It
requires religious courage to rejoice.
—Soren Kierkegaard

But ye, beloved, building up yourselves on your most holy faith, praying in the Holy Ghost, Keep yourselves in the love of God, looking for the mercy of our Lord Jesus Christ unto eternal life.

—Jude 1:20-21

Sometimes, I think, the things we see
are shadows of the things to be;
that what we plan we build;
that every hope that hath been crossed,
and every dream we thought was lost,
in heaven shall be fulfilled.
—Phoebe Cary

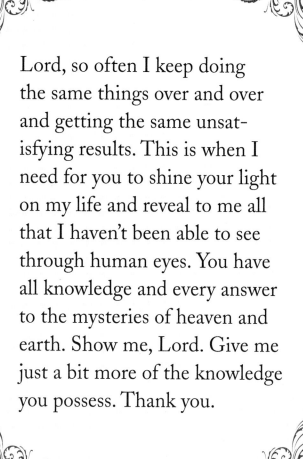

Lord, so often I keep doing the same things over and over and getting the same unsatisfying results. This is when I need for you to shine your light on my life and reveal to me all that I haven't been able to see through human eyes. You have all knowledge and every answer to the mysteries of heaven and earth. Show me, Lord. Give me just a bit more of the knowledge you possess. Thank you.

Walk in wisdom toward them that are without, redeeming the time. Let your speech be always with grace, seasoned with salt, that ye may know how ye ought to answer every man.

—Colossians 4:5-6

There are times in everyone's life when something constructive is born out of adversity...when things seem so bad that you've got to grab your fate by the shoulders and shake it.
—Author unknown

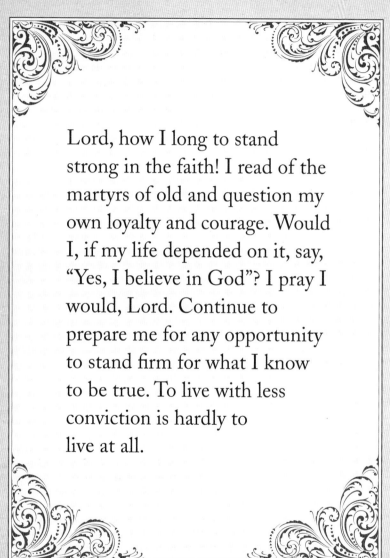

Lord, how I long to stand strong in the faith! I read of the martyrs of old and question my own loyalty and courage. Would I, if my life depended on it, say, "Yes, I believe in God"? I pray I would, Lord. Continue to prepare me for any opportunity to stand firm for what I know to be true. To live with less conviction is hardly to live at all.

*I acknowledge my sin unto thee,
and mine iniquity have I not hid.
I said, I will confess my transgressions
unto the Lord;
and thou forgavest the iniquity of my
sin. Selah*

—Psalm 32:5

Forgiveness is the fragrance the violet
sheds on the heel that has crushed it.
—Mark Twain

Wait on the Lord: be of good courage, and he shall strengthen thine heart: wait, I say, on the Lord.

—Psalm 27:14

Love has hands to help others. It has feet to hasten to the poor and needy. It has eyes to see misery and want. It has ears to hear the sighs and sorrows of men. This is what love looks like.
—St. Augustine

That their hearts might be comforted, being knit together in love, and unto all riches of the full assurance of understanding, to the acknowledgement of the mystery of God, and of the Father, and of Christ.

—Colossians 2:2

One word frees us of all the weight and pain in life. That word is love.
—Sophocles

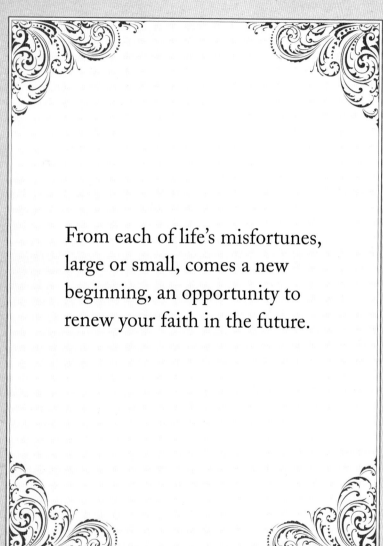

From each of life's misfortunes, large or small, comes a new beginning, an opportunity to renew your faith in the future.

Miracles are not contrary
to nature, but only
contrary to what we
know about nature.
—Augustine of Hippo

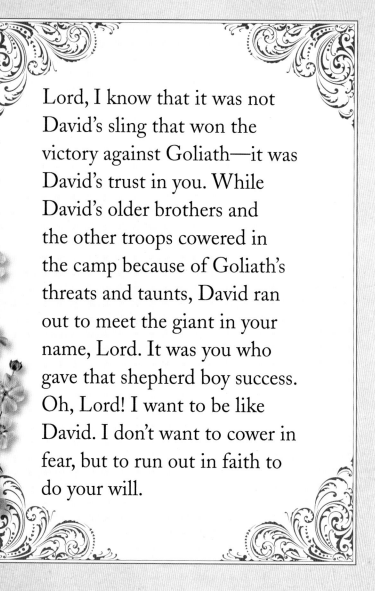

Lord, I know that it was not David's sling that won the victory against Goliath—it was David's trust in you. While David's older brothers and the other troops cowered in the camp because of Goliath's threats and taunts, David ran out to meet the giant in your name, Lord. It was you who gave that shepherd boy success. Oh, Lord! I want to be like David. I don't want to cower in fear, but to run out in faith to do your will.

*Behold, how good and
how pleasant it is
for brethren to dwell together
in unity!*

—Psalm 133:1

Into thy hands, O Father and Lord, we commend this night, ourselves, our families and friends, all those we love and those who love us, all folk rightly believing, and all who need thy pity and protection: light us with thy holy grace, and suffer us never to be separated from thee, O Lord in Trinity, God everlasting.
—St. Edmund Rich,
Archbishop of Canterbury

August

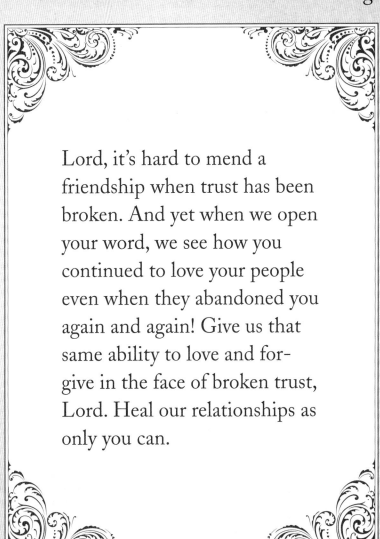

Lord, it's hard to mend a friendship when trust has been broken. And yet when we open your word, we see how you continued to love your people even when they abandoned you again and again! Give us that same ability to love and forgive in the face of broken trust, Lord. Heal our relationships as only you can.

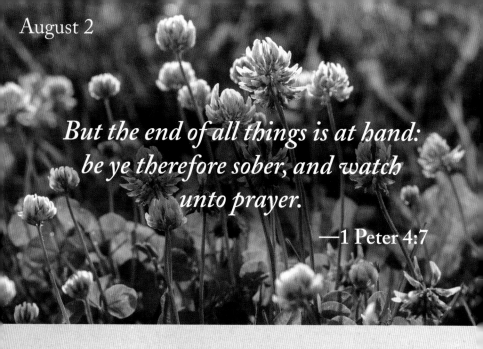

*But the end of all things is at hand:
be ye therefore sober, and watch
unto prayer.*

—1 Peter 4:7

Lord, on days when everything seems to go wrong, help me to remember that you are always nearby to offer comfort. It is easy to get overwhelmed and feel lost and alone in this world, but deep down I know that is never the case. You are always at the ready to help—I just need to remember to take a moment to stop, breathe, and pray.

Lord, sometimes my past rises up to haunt me—or worse yet, to bite me. These are the real-world consequences of poor choices I've made. But even though I'm reminded of them because of the cause-and-effect nature of things, once I confess them to you and receive your forgiveness, they are erased from your record book. While consequences may linger, your forgiveness is complete. Thank you for that eternal reality.

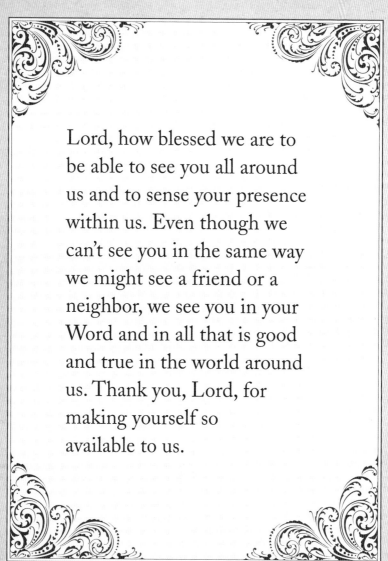

Lord, how blessed we are to be able to see you all around us and to sense your presence within us. Even though we can't see you in the same way we might see a friend or a neighbor, we see you in your Word and in all that is good and true in the world around us. Thank you, Lord, for making yourself so available to us.

Blessed are they that mourn:
for they shall be comforted.

—Matthew 5:4

Lord, what comfort we find in your
changeless nature. When we look back
and remember all the ways you've guided
us in the past, we know we have no need
to be anxious about the future. You were,
are, and always will be our Savior and
Lord. Why should we fear instability
when you are always here with us?

Like aching bones that find
relief in a steamy, hot bath, O
God, that's the comfort I long
for. Take from my life
the fear, the hurt, the doubt,
the unknown, the insecurity—
the afflictions. Nonetheless,
your promise is to comfort us
in our afflictions not remove
them. Help me to know that
I will experience the "relief" I
want only when I am open to
accepting your healing
comfort that gives us the
strength to triumph.

Lord, thank you for calling me to yourself and then giving me your spirit to strengthen me—heart, soul, mind, and body—to work in ways that bring honor to you. This goal of being a model of good works in every respect makes me realize how much I need you each moment. And as I grow in a life of doing what is right and true and good, help me grow in humility as well, re-membering that you are the source of my strength.

But when the Comforter is come,
whom I will send unto you from
the Father, even the Spirit of truth,
which proceedeth from the Father,
he shall testify of me.

—John 15:26

Lord, how we cling to your promise that
the Holy Spirit is always near to all who
believe in you. How comforting it is for us
as parents to know that our children have
the Holy Spirit to guide them and lead
them into a purposeful life. We praise you,
Lord, for your loving care for us and for
our children and grandchildren.

But every man hath his proper gift of God, one after this manner, and another after that.

—1 Corinthians 7:7

What a wonderful day! And now, God of rest and peace, the children are sleeping, replete with the joys of our summer discoveries that they are savoring to the last drop. We celebrate the joy of ordinary days and rest in your care.

And be ye kind one to another, tenderhearted, forgiving one another, even as God for Christ's sake hath forgiven you.

—Ephesians 4:32

O Lord, when you promise us you have removed our sins from us, why do we dredge them up so we can wallow in regret and shame all over again? Keep us from wasting time and energy thinking about past mistakes, Lord. If they are no longer on your radar, they surely don't belong on ours. How blessed we are to have such a compassionate, forgiving God!

> *It is of the Lord's mercies that we are not consumed,*
> *because his compassions fail not.*
> *They are new every morning:*
> *great is thy faithfulness.*
> —Lamentations 3:22-23

When I leave you behind and try to go about my day without your guidance, Lord, it's like groping around in the dark. I stub my heart on relational issues. I trip over my ego. I bump into walls of frustration. I fall down the steps of my foolish choices. How much better to seek the light of your presence first thing and enjoy the benefit of having you illuminate each step of my day!

Finally, be ye all of one mind, having compassion one of another, love as brethren, be pitiful, be courteous.

—1 Peter 3:8

Lord, today I ask you to slow me down and open my ears so I will notice the needs of those around me. Too often I breeze by people with an offhand greeting but remain in a cocoon of my own concerns. I know many around me are hurting, Lord. Help me find ways to be of service.

Then came Peter to him, and said, Lord, how oft shall my brother sin against me, and I forgive him? till seven times? Jesus saith unto him, I say not unto thee, Until seven times: but, Until seventy times seven.

—Matthew 18:21-22

Forgiveness is a supernatural response to being wronged. Would we know what forgiveness is if God had not shown us by first forgiving us? It seems highly unlikely. That's why real forgiveness—the kind that God extends to us—can only come through God's grace.

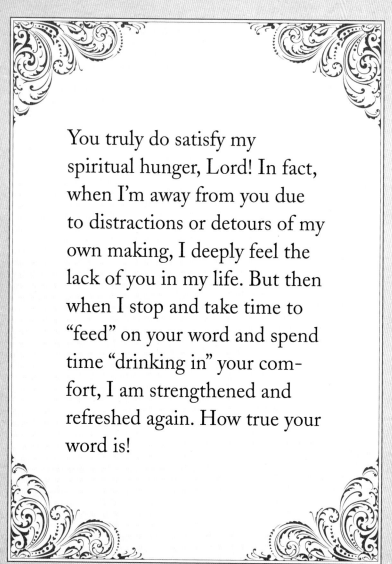

You truly do satisfy my spiritual hunger, Lord! In fact, when I'm away from you due to distractions or detours of my own making, I deeply feel the lack of you in my life. But then when I stop and take time to "feed" on your word and spend time "drinking in" your comfort, I am strengthened and refreshed again. How true your word is!

And therefore will the Lord wait,
that he may be gracious unto you,
and therefore will he be exalted,
that he may have mercy upon you:
for the Lord is a God of judgment:
blessed are all they that wait for him.

—Isaiah 30:18

Often we rush ahead with a plan we think is from you only to watch it end in disaster. At these times we know we moved too fast. Yet we don't want to lack the faith to move forward when necessary! Give us wisdom and discernment, Lord.

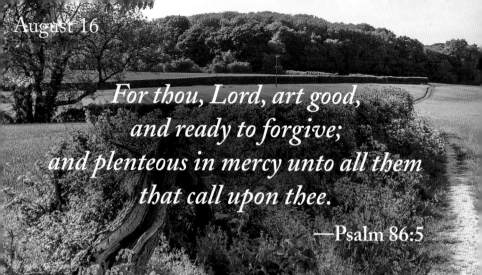

For thou, Lord, art good,
and ready to forgive;
and plenteous in mercy unto all them
that call upon thee.

—Psalm 86:5

Instead of choosing retaliation or revenge,
we can extend love and compassion.
This doesn't mean that we coddle them
or fail to confront any hurtful ways, but
it does mean that even as we hold them
accountable, we don't withhold our love.

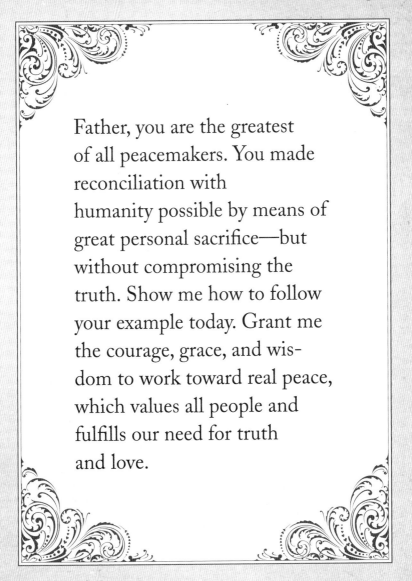

Father, you are the greatest of all peacemakers. You made reconciliation with humanity possible by means of great personal sacrifice—but without compromising the truth. Show me how to follow your example today. Grant me the courage, grace, and wisdom to work toward real peace, which values all people and fulfills our need for truth and love.

And rend your heart,
and not your garments,
and turn unto the Lord your God:
for he is gracious and merciful,
slow to anger, and of great kindness,
and repenteth him of the evil.

—Joel 2:13

God of all comfort, have mercy on me.
I need your comforting strength, dear
God, wrapped around me like a soothing
blanket, so that I can ask my family for
forgiveness. Bless me with more patience,
too, so that we don't have to go through all
this again tomorrow. Thank you, God.

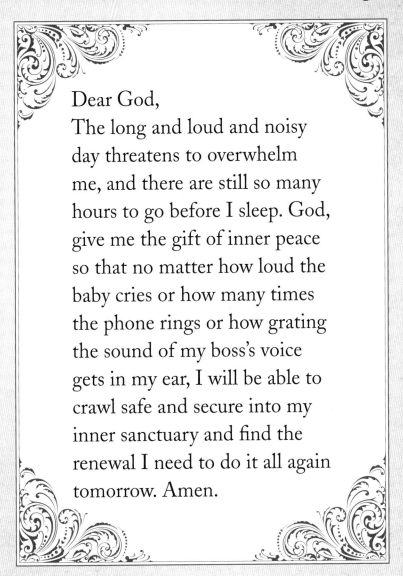

Dear God,
The long and loud and noisy day threatens to overwhelm me, and there are still so many hours to go before I sleep. God, give me the gift of inner peace so that no matter how loud the baby cries or how many times the phone rings or how grating the sound of my boss's voice gets in my ear, I will be able to crawl safe and secure into my inner sanctuary and find the renewal I need to do it all again tomorrow. Amen.

How do we pick up the pieces and go on when our hearts ache as they never have before?

O Lord, it is so hard to see the hope in certain circumstances. I guess we just need time. Time to grieve. Time to regain our balance. Time to renew our trust and hope for the future. While we are going through this season of healing, please hold us close.

The grace of the Lord Jesus Christ, and the love of God, and the communion of the Holy Ghost, be with you all. Amen.

—2 Corinthians 13:14

Lord, let me be strong today, drawing my courage from my hope in you. Help me lean not on my own strength but on your limitless power. I know there is work to be done—burdens to be lifted, temptations to be resisted, unkindness to be forgiven. Let my thoughts and actions be motivated by the hope generated by your promises.

I feel free in your love, God.
I feel as if I can live free from
others' opinions, free from
guilt, and free from fear
because no matter what,
your love is there for me. But
I know that freedom can be
abused, so help me
remember that I also have been
freed from the tyranny of fear,
hatred, and arrogance. Show
me how to remain free and to
lead others into your sanctuary
of peace and freedom. Amen.

Lord, you are the foundation of my life. When circumstances shift and make my world unsteady, you remain firm. When threats of what lies ahead blow against the framework of my thoughts, you are solid. When I focus on your steadfastness, I realize that you are my strength for the moment, the one sure thing in my life. Because of you I stand now, and I will stand tomorrow as well, because you are there already. Amen.

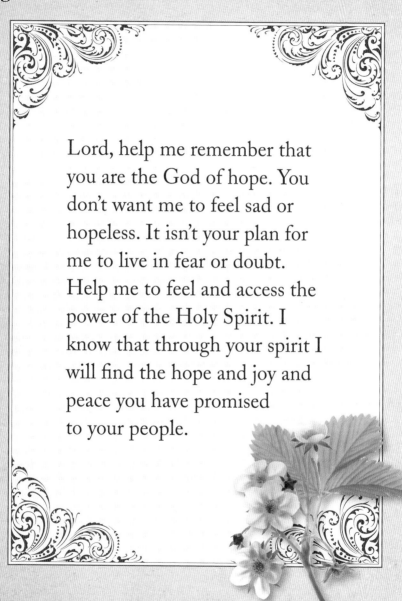

Lord, help me remember that you are the God of hope. You don't want me to feel sad or hopeless. It isn't your plan for me to live in fear or doubt. Help me to feel and access the power of the Holy Spirit. I know that through your spirit I will find the hope and joy and peace you have promised to your people.

Lord, be my warrior, my guard, my guide. Let your love be the armor that shields me from the slings and arrows of the day. Let your compassion be the blanket that protects me from the cold at night. Lord, be my warrior, my champion, my protector. Let your love surround me like an impenetrable light that nothing can break through to do me harm. Let your grace bring me peace no matter how crazy things are all around me. Lord, be my warrior.

God, when I am tired and just feeling down about everything in my life, your love reminds me that there is a spring of hope and renewal I can drink from anytime. It may take me awhile to come around, but I always come back to love as the reason to keep on going, even when my gas tank is empty. Love fuels me and gets me back out on the road of life, ready for whatever new challenge you have in store for me.

No greater blessing exists than the feeling of being where we belong, with the people who make us happy, in the homes that bring us comfort and a sense of peace, doing work that makes us feel needed and satisfied. When we find our "true north," we feel at home and blessings await us behind each and every door.

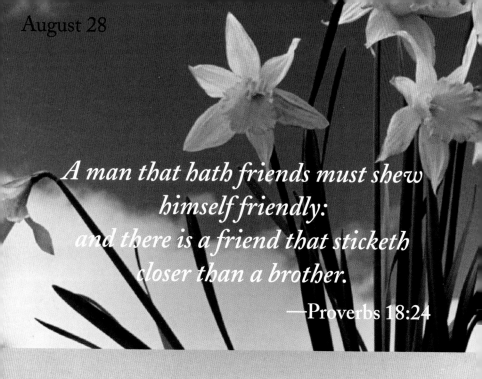

*A man that hath friends must shew
himself friendly:
and there is a friend that sticketh
closer than a brother.*

—Proverbs 18:24

Dear heavenly Father, today, if I see or
hear of someone who is struggling in
some way, please help me take a moment
to remember what it was like when I was
struggling and you helped me through
the aid of a friend or stranger. Let that
memory mobilize me to offer help and be
your true servant. This I pray. Amen.

Thank you, Lord, for the
signs of your power. Thank
you for the awe I feel during a
thunderstorm or at the sight of
a monument in nature. Thank
you for the thrill I feel when I
see one of your works in all its
glory. It is good to know your
power and feel its presence
in my life.

The Lord is my light and my salvation; whom shall I fear? the Lord is the strength of my life; of whom shall I be afraid?

—Psalm 27:1

Natural light holds a lot of sway. As it changes throughout the day, our attitudes, our way of engaging, can be affected. Some people crave the uplift of natural light, and miss it when the seasons turn or storms blow through. And sunlight can positively affect our physical selves, providing vitamin D essential to good health. We recognize the beauty and power of light!

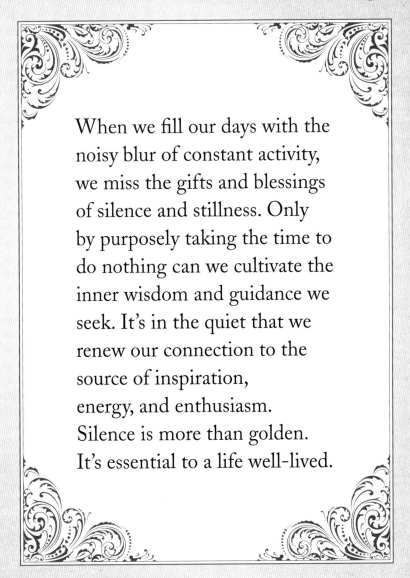

When we fill our days with the
noisy blur of constant activity,
we miss the gifts and blessings
of silence and stillness. Only
by purposely taking the time to
do nothing can we cultivate the
inner wisdom and guidance we
seek. It's in the quiet that we
renew our connection to the
source of inspiration,
energy, and enthusiasm.
Silence is more than golden.
It's essential to a life well-lived.

September

Ye are the light of the world. A city that is set on an hill cannot be hid.

—Matthew 5:14

No matter what is going on outside of us, hope is that quiet whisper within that gives us the strength and courage to keep going. The ways of the world may be chaotic, loud, and distracting, but we can keep a sense of inner calm when our hope is centered in God's eternal presence. Hope is our anchor to the rock of God's love when we feel tossed and turned upon the waves of life.

259

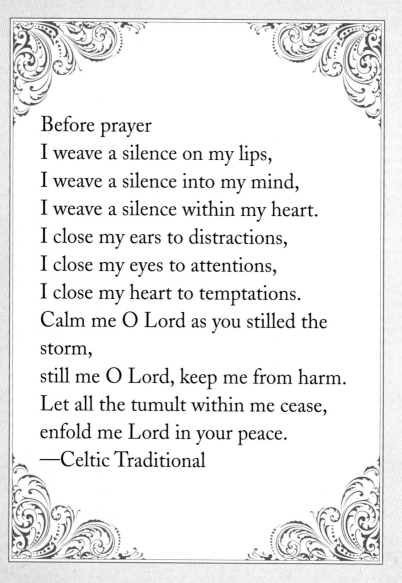

Before prayer
I weave a silence on my lips,
I weave a silence into my mind,
I weave a silence within my heart.
I close my ears to distractions,
I close my eyes to attentions,
I close my heart to temptations.
Calm me O Lord as you stilled the
storm,
still me O Lord, keep me from harm.
Let all the tumult within me cease,
enfold me Lord in your peace.
—Celtic Traditional

*Honour thy father and thy mother:
that thy days may be long upon
the land which the Lord thy God
giveth thee.*

—Exodus 20:12

If I put my hope in people, I am often
disappointed.
If I put my hope in circumstances, I am
often let down.
But when I put my hope in God, I am
always taken care of.
God is my rock and my hope, in him is a
firm foundation from which I live my life.

The promise of hope fills the heart with a new perspective, and the eyes with a new vision. Darkness begins to lift, showing the path we could not see before, and a way out of our pain and suffering. The promise of hope opens doors we were certain were closed, and reveals solutions that evaded us. Hope is a key that unlocks the way to the blessings of God around us.

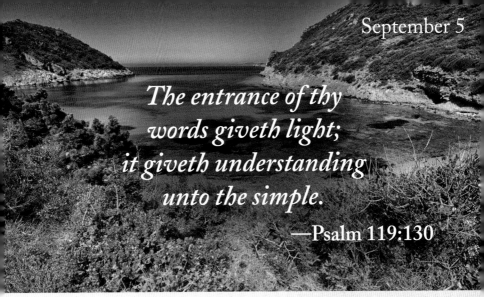

The entrance of thy words giveth light; it giveth understanding unto the simple.

—Psalm 119:130

I cannot see the light, but I know it is just up ahead. I cannot find the way out, but I know that my path is leading me there. I cannot solve the problem, but I know the solution is on its way. I know these things because of my faith in God, who has never failed me, and never will.

Take comfort in God's
steadfast presence.
Even when you suffer,
take comfort
in the hope of God's healing.
Even when you fear,
take comfort
in the hope of God's strength.
No matter what you face,
take comfort
in knowing you never
walk alone.

Hast thou not known?
hast thou not heard,
that the everlasting God, the Lord,
the Creator of the ends of the earth,
fainteth not, neither is weary?
there is no searching
of his understanding.

—Isaiah 40:28

Lean on your faith when there is no one around to help. Like a strong pillar, faith in God can hold you up during the worst of storms and the harshest of winds. Faith gives you something to hold onto. Faith even brings you back home to God again when you are sure you are lost and alone.

265

To have hope is to put our life into the hands of a loving God that is always looking out for us, always making clear our path. When we are feeling down and about to give up, hope is like the sign on the road that tells us "rest stop ahead," and suddenly we feel renewed and refreshed, able to walk on just a bit longer and just a bit farther than we thought we could alone.

This then is the message which we have heard of him, and declare unto you, that God is light, and in him is no darkness at all.

—1 John 1:5

We all have days when nothing goes right, and all we want to do is crawl back to bed and curl up into a ball. Sometimes those days stretch into weeks and months of bleak depression. But God is always there, watching over us, gently urging us to have hope because He has a plan for us. We may not see it unfolding, but it is, and hope is the pathway there.

What does it mean to have faith? It means moving through the challenges of daily life with boldness because we know that someone has our back. It means approaching life's obstacles with courage and conviction because we know someone is looking out for us. It means walking with our heads held high because we know someone walks with us. That someone is God.

This is a sad and solemn day, yet there is still time to be thankful. Thank you, Lord, for all the emergency workers who help people every day. They bring light to the darkness and help to those who need it most. Thank you for their selflessness and willingness to give everything they have to save another. Just as Jesus sacrificed his life to save us, we are blessed by the sacrifices of those who save our lives.

September 12

I thank thee, and praise thee,
O thou God of my fathers,
who hast given me wisdom and might,
and hast made known unto me now
what we desired of thee:
for thou hast now made known unto us
the king's matter.

—Daniel 2:23

To have faith is to have the promise
of God's love to see you through any
situation in life. Faith accompanies us,
helping us to see the next step along the
unseen path that is his will. When we step
out of faith, we step away from the peace
and comfort of God. Walking in faith is
walking with God.

All things are possible to those who have faith. Putting our trust in God gives us wings to soar higher, dream bigger, and go farther than we thought we ever could. We rest in faith, like a comfortable chair, relaxed in the knowing that whatever we need will be given to us in God's due time. What a wonderful feeling, to have an unshakeable faith and an immovable trust in his will for us!

Imagine having the arms of a loving, caring angel wrapped around you when you are sad or upset. Faith is like that. Comforting and encouraging, faith is like a trustworthy old friend that is never too tired or busy to hear your problems or help you find your footing again when you stumble through life. Faith in God is our best friend and ally.

Every good gift and every perfect gift is from above, and cometh down from the Father of lights, with whom is no variableness, neither shadow of turning.

—James 1:17

When I can see no way out of the dark tunnel of despair, my faith becomes the bright beacon of light that guides my path. When I can feel no end to the pain I am suffering, my faith becomes the soothing balm that brings relief. My faith in God never disappoints me or abandons me. Even though I cannot see it, I know it is always at work in my life.

A heart in pain from disappointment can't always see the love that already surrounds it. That love is ever-present because it comes from God, who never abandons us. The love of God is steady and true, even when we think nobody cares about us. God does, now and forever. Opening our hearts to God is the beginning of healing, and the end of pain and suffering. God's love abides in us...always.

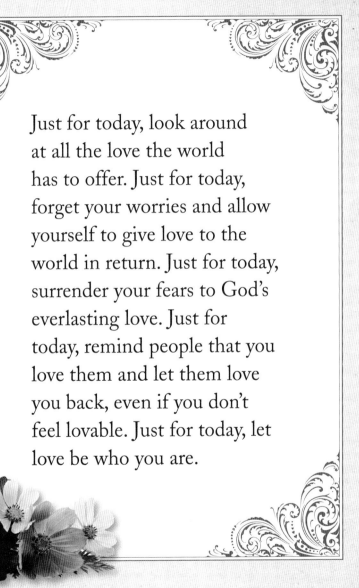

Just for today, look around
at all the love the world
has to offer. Just for today,
forget your worries and allow
yourself to give love to the
world in return. Just for today,
surrender your fears to God's
everlasting love. Just for
today, remind people that you
love them and let them love
you back, even if you don't
feel lovable. Just for today, let
love be who you are.

We may be surrounded by friends and family, yet still feel so alone and misunderstood. Those around us may have their own problems and worries, leaving us feeling abandoned and unseen. But we are never truly alone, for God is always present. God's love is unceasing and unfailing, and we don't have to ask for it, or wait in line for it. We may forget God, but God never forgets us.

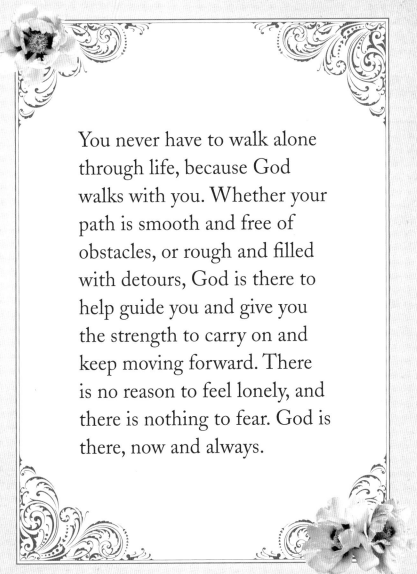

You never have to walk alone through life, because God walks with you. Whether your path is smooth and free of obstacles, or rough and filled with detours, God is there to help guide you and give you the strength to carry on and keep moving forward. There is no reason to feel lonely, and there is nothing to fear. God is there, now and always.

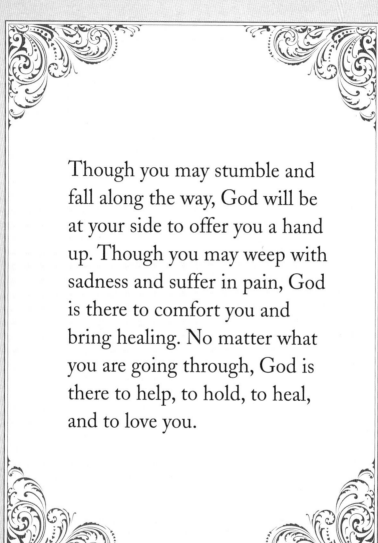

Though you may stumble and fall along the way, God will be at your side to offer you a hand up. Though you may weep with sadness and suffer in pain, God is there to comfort you and bring healing. No matter what you are going through, God is there to help, to hold, to heal, and to love you.

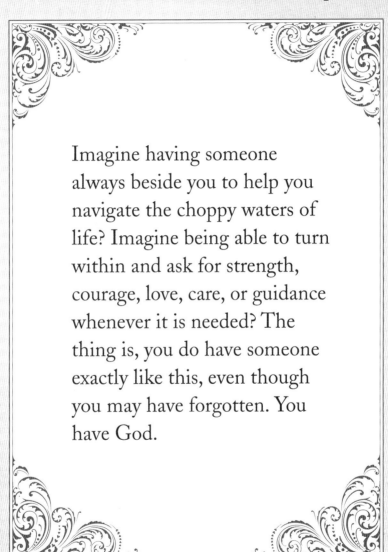

Imagine having someone always beside you to help you navigate the choppy waters of life? Imagine being able to turn within and ask for strength, courage, love, care, or guidance whenever it is needed? The thing is, you do have someone exactly like this, even though you may have forgotten. You have God.

An hypocrite with his mouth destroyeth his neighbour: but through knowledge shall the just be delivered.

—Proverbs 11:9

Friends come and go, but God remains. Life is filled with relationships between friends, family, and loved ones. Some of those will last a season or two, some may last forever. But the one true friendship we will never lose is the one we have with God. The presence of God does not come and go like the tides of the ocean. The presence of God is forever.

When all is said and done, God remains. Love interests will leave us, family and friends will move away or pass on, and our children will grow to have lives of their own. Even our pets will one day be gone. But there is no reason to feel alone, or lonely, because God remains to walk with us on life's journey. God's presence has no shelf life or expiration date.

Turn you at my reproof:
behold, I will pour out my
spirit unto you,
I will make known my
words unto you.

—**Proverbs 1:23**

Within the heart, where the spirit dwells, is the still, small voice of God speaking to us. The voice is never silent. Instead, we are often distracted by the chaotic noises of life to hear it. The voice is always there when we are ready to look inside, and listen to what he is trying to tell us. God speaks to us all the time. Our job is to quiet the mind long enough to hear him.

That the God of our Lord Jesus Christ, the Father of glory, may give unto you the spirit of wisdom and revelation in the knowledge of him.

—Ephesians 1:17

There is no greater comfort to a broken spirit than the love of God. There is no more soothing a balm to heal the wounds of a suffering soul than the love of God. There is no deeper peace to be found for a restless heart than the love of God.

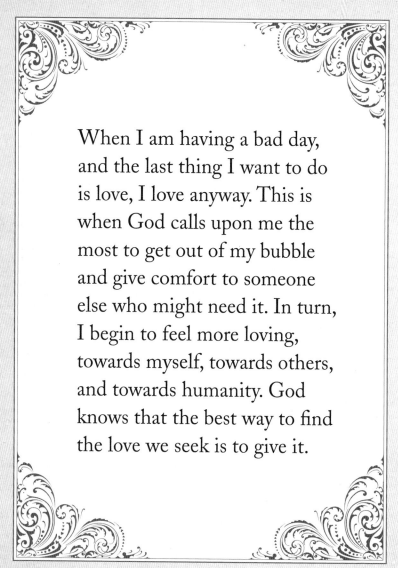

When I am having a bad day, and the last thing I want to do is love, I love anyway. This is when God calls upon me the most to get out of my bubble and give comfort to someone else who might need it. In turn, I begin to feel more loving, towards myself, towards others, and towards humanity. God knows that the best way to find the love we seek is to give it.

Loneliness can sometimes feel like a thick, heavy fog blocking out the warm sun and blue sky. But remembering that God loves me helps clear away the fog and gives me a new sense of clarity and direction. Even if people cannot find time for me, God is always there, unfailing in his love and steadfast care.

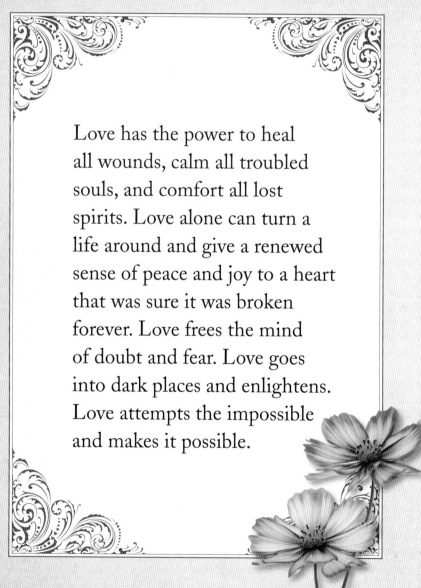

Love has the power to heal
all wounds, calm all troubled
souls, and comfort all lost
spirits. Love alone can turn a
life around and give a renewed
sense of peace and joy to a heart
that was sure it was broken
forever. Love frees the mind
of doubt and fear. Love goes
into dark places and enlightens.
Love attempts the impossible
and makes it possible.

The world is filled with unloving people, but God asks that we love them anyway. It does no good to meet hatred with more hatred, so God asks that we meet hatred with love. The more good we can put into the world, the better our world will be, and soon that goodness will spread like wildfire, changing cold hearts to warm, and lost souls to found again. That is the power of love.

Therefore whatsoever ye have spoken in darkness shall be heard in the light; and that which ye have spoken in the ear in closets shall be proclaimed upon the housetops.

—Luke 12:3

Hope is a soft, warm blanket that comforts us when we are cold, wrapping itself around our weary bones and giving us the promise of better times to come. Hope embraces us in arms of love and care, renewing our broken spirits with the reminder that this too shall pass.

October

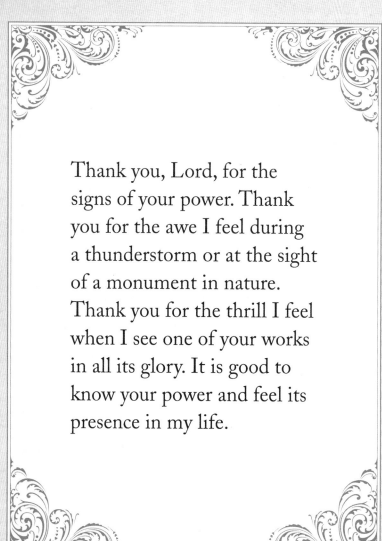

Thank you, Lord, for the signs of your power. Thank you for the awe I feel during a thunderstorm or at the sight of a monument in nature. Thank you for the thrill I feel when I see one of your works in all its glory. It is good to know your power and feel its presence in my life.

*When thou passest through the waters,
I will be with thee;
and through the rivers,
they shall not overflow thee:
when thou walkest through the fire,
thou shalt not be burned;
neither shall the flame kindle upon thee.*

—Isaiah 43:2

God comforts me with his love when I am feeling cold and alone. God warms me with his loving care when I am feeling neglected. God sees me when I am feeling unseen, and reminds me of my worth when I am feeling inadequate. God's love is my comfort in all things, and it makes me whole again.

For I the Lord thy God
will hold thy right hand,
saying unto thee, Fear not;
I will help thee.

—Isaiah 41:13

How often do we let time drift by without telling those we hold dear to us how much we love them? How often do we fear speaking words of love because we might be rejected? If only we could possibly know just how much we are loved, by each other, and by God. We would then know that miracles truly exist and all things are possible. Love gives us wings. Tell someone you love them today.

But the God of all grace, who hath called us unto his eternal glory by Christ Jesus, after that ye have suffered a while, make you perfect, stablish, strengthen, settle you.

—1 Peter 5:10

Grace is the presence of God at work in your life. It shows itself in the form of people and events that come into your orbit just when you need them. Small miracles and happy coincidences are proof that God is always showering grace down upon you. Just open your eyes, and your heart, and you will see it everywhere.

I know that when I am sad, lonely, and afraid, I can turn to God for his loving grace. With mercy and compassion, God hears my cries and comes to my aid, ready to take away my burdens and heal my wounded heart. He gives me wisdom and understanding, and helps me to forgive those who have hurt me. God's unceasing love for me is what grace is all about.

Surrender to the grace of a loving God. Give up your worries and concerns, your fears and doubts, to a God that cares and won't let you down. Turn over your challenges and obstacles to a God who makes your way clear and smooth again. When life becomes a struggle, give up the fight and give in to the grace of a power greater and wiser than yourself.

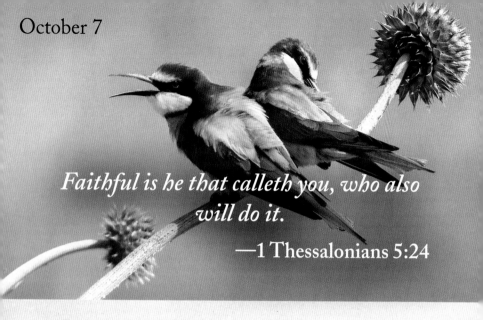

Faithful is he that calleth you, who also will do it.

—1 Thessalonians 5:24

We think of grace as God's favor upon us, but God is always favoring every single one of us. Grace is the acceptance of that favor, allowing it to flow through our days and nights, bringing the gifts of a loving God to us whenever we need it. Grace, like God, is a door through which we must first walk to enter a room filled with blessings, love, and joy.

There but for the grace
of God go I. God is my
protection, and my guardian.
I know that I am always being
watched over and blessed
because that is God's promise
to me. I walk in grace, and
offer it to those I meet along
the way. I stand in grace,
letting it surround me with a
love that is eternal and
forgiving of all my sins.

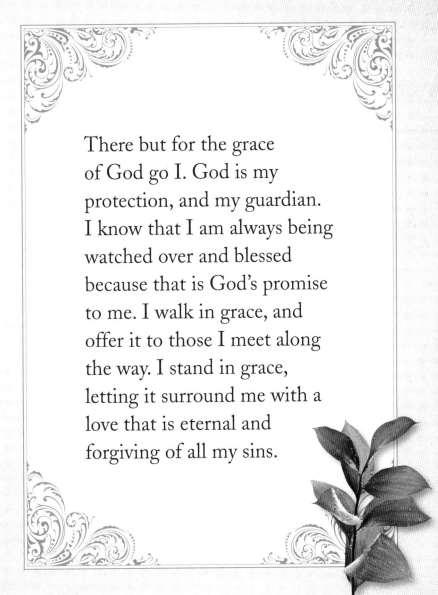

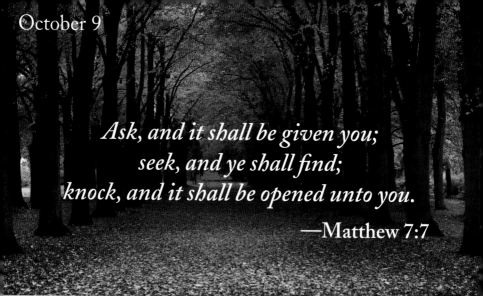

Ask, and it shall be given you;
seek, and ye shall find;
knock, and it shall be opened unto you.

—Matthew 7:7

No matter what mistakes you have made, God is ready to show favor upon you. No matter how much you have messed up your life, God is ready with love and understanding to help you reclaim what was lost. No matter how sad or depressed you may be feeling, God is ready to wrap you in arms of loving grace and make you feel cared for again.

Have you ever felt the power of God's amazing grace? Have you ever tasted the sweetness of God's merciful forgiveness? Have you ever heard God's kind words of understanding and support? You will know it when you do, for all darkness will be made light, and all suffering will give way to a new joyfulness and inner peace. This is the power of God's amazing grace.

I may not know what the next step is, but God does. I may not understand why I am going through a particular challenge, but God does. The wisdom of God knows all and sees the bigger picture, when I am only able to grasp a small piece of the puzzle. I put my trust and faith in God's greater vision for my life and allow it to unfold according to his will.

Whereby are given unto us exceeding great and precious promises: that by these ye might be partakers of the divine nature, having escaped the corruption that is in the world through lust.

—2 Peter 1:4

What we cannot do for ourselves, God can do for us. With our limited vision and perception, only God's wisdom can look beyond our lack and limitations. How comforting is it to know that we have this resource to turn to anytime we need? God is always ready to help us, to advise us, and to direct us.

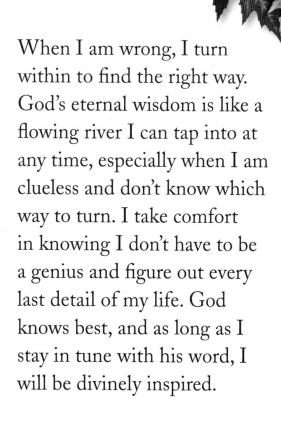

When I am wrong, I turn within to find the right way. God's eternal wisdom is like a flowing river I can tap into at any time, especially when I am clueless and don't know which way to turn. I take comfort in knowing I don't have to be a genius and figure out every last detail of my life. God knows best, and as long as I stay in tune with his word, I will be divinely inspired.

This world is full of people who have to be right, even if it means losing friendships or family connections. The need to be right causes so much suffering. Instead, seek the need to be wise. Seek the ability to use your God-given wisdom to be of help to others, and not a burden. No one is right all the time, and it takes wisdom to realize that and to learn to be compassionate to others, and to yourself.

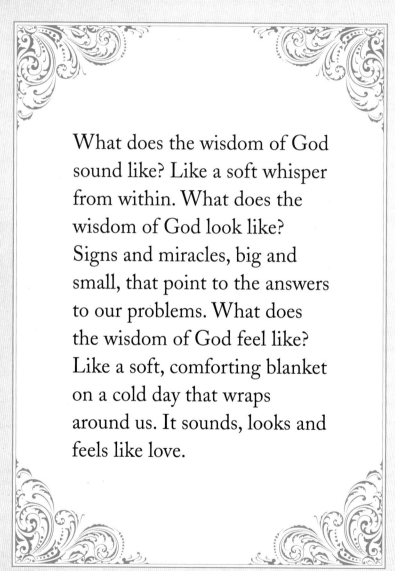

What does the wisdom of God
sound like? Like a soft whisper
from within. What does the
wisdom of God look like?
Signs and miracles, big and
small, that point to the answers
to our problems. What does
the wisdom of God feel like?
Like a soft, comforting blanket
on a cold day that wraps
around us. It sounds, looks and
feels like love.

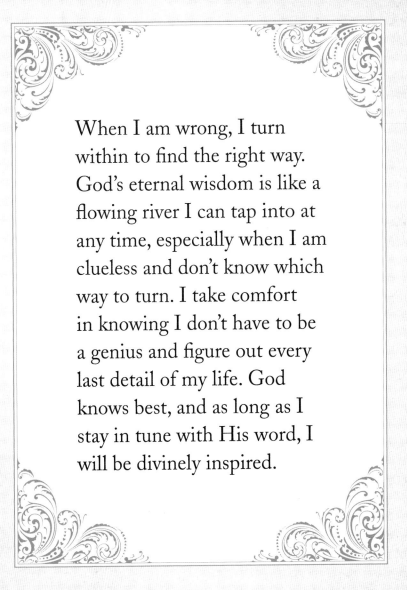

When I am wrong, I turn within to find the right way. God's eternal wisdom is like a flowing river I can tap into at any time, especially when I am clueless and don't know which way to turn. I take comfort in knowing I don't have to be a genius and figure out every last detail of my life. God knows best, and as long as I stay in tune with His word, I will be divinely inspired.

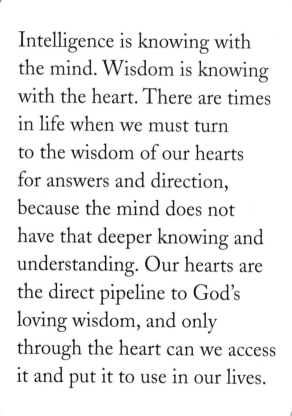

Intelligence is knowing with the mind. Wisdom is knowing with the heart. There are times in life when we must turn to the wisdom of our hearts for answers and direction, because the mind does not have that deeper knowing and understanding. Our hearts are the direct pipeline to God's loving wisdom, and only through the heart can we access it and put it to use in our lives.

And for this cause he is the mediator of the new testament, that by means of death, for the redemption of the transgressions that were under the first testament, they which are called might receive the promise of eternal inheritance.

—Hebrews 9:15

I am to forgive those who sin against me. This is hard to do, because it's so much easier to hold onto grudges and resentments. I feel that I was right and just, and that they hurt me. But until I can let go of that, I will never be free to be happy. God forgives me, and I must forgive others in return.

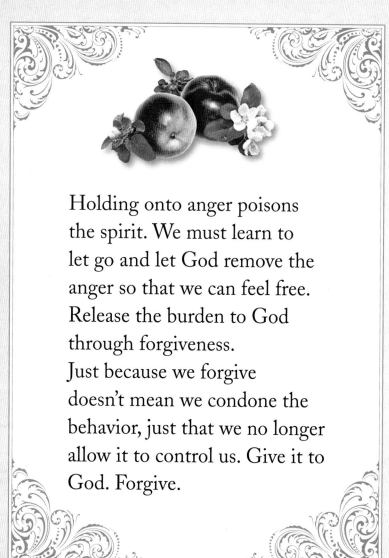

Holding onto anger poisons the spirit. We must learn to let go and let God remove the anger so that we can feel free. Release the burden to God through forgiveness.

Just because we forgive doesn't mean we condone the behavior, just that we no longer allow it to control us. Give it to God. Forgive.

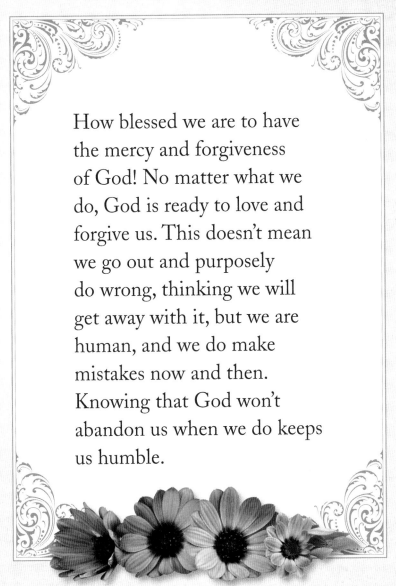

How blessed we are to have the mercy and forgiveness of God! No matter what we do, God is ready to love and forgive us. This doesn't mean we go out and purposely do wrong, thinking we will get away with it, but we are human, and we do make mistakes now and then. Knowing that God won't abandon us when we do keeps us humble.

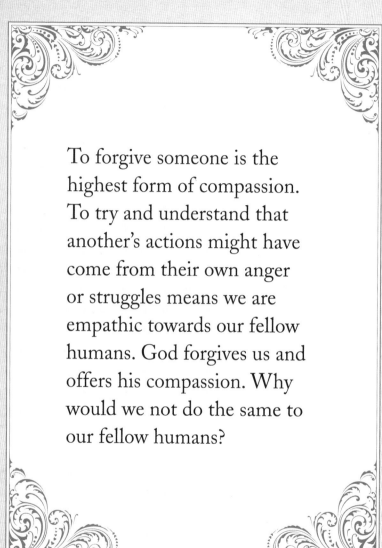

To forgive someone is the highest form of compassion. To try and understand that another's actions might have come from their own anger or struggles means we are empathic towards our fellow humans. God forgives us and offers his compassion. Why would we not do the same to our fellow humans?

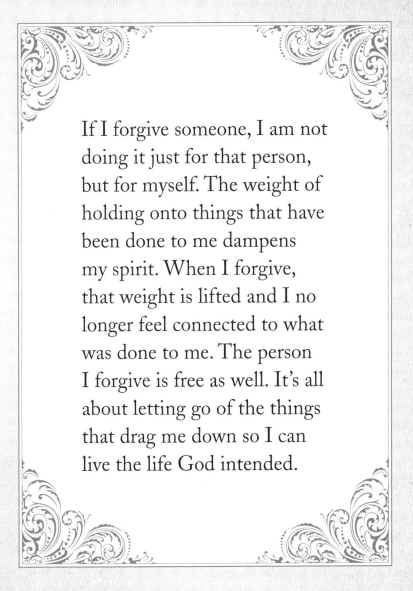

If I forgive someone, I am not doing it just for that person, but for myself. The weight of holding onto things that have been done to me dampens my spirit. When I forgive, that weight is lifted and I no longer feel connected to what was done to me. The person I forgive is free as well. It's all about letting go of the things that drag me down so I can live the life God intended.

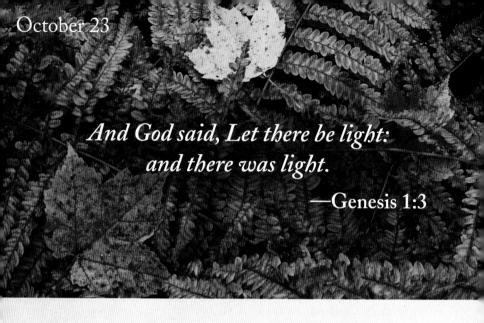

And God said, Let there be light: and there was light.

—Genesis 1:3

We have all been hurt in life. We have all been at the receiving end of another's wrath or anger. Even if that person never apologizes, we must still forgive. Do we want to live our lives holding onto the actions of another? Do we want to feel the tension of another person's behaviors towards us? It is only when we forgive that we can once again feel light and loving and kind.

*The Lord thy God in the midst of
thee is mighty; he will save,
he will rejoice over thee with joy;
he will rest in his love,
he will joy over thee with singing.*

—Zephaniah 3:17

Do not worry about the regrets of the
past. God forgives you. Do not stress
over a wrong word or a misguided action.
God forgives you. Do not cry over a
bad decision or a terrible mistake. God
forgives you. Learn the lessons from your
actions, then turn to God and know that
he loves you and forgives you. Then strive
to do better the next time.

But if from thence thou shalt seek the Lord thy God, thou shalt find him, if thou seek him with all thy heart and with all thy soul.

—Deuteronomy 4:29

The brave and compassionate soul can forgive the most horrible of crimes. With God's love and guidance, we can forgive much less. People hurt people, and God asks that we look beyond the surface of things to the deeper truth. We are all God's children, even those that do terrible things, sometimes causing us tremendous pain and suffering. Forgive them anyway.

Have not I commanded thee? Be strong and of a good courage; be not afraid, neither be thou dismayed: for the Lord thy God is with thee whithersoever thou goest.

—Joshua 1:9

Life is filled with experiences that require us to reach deep within and find our courage. When fear threatens to keep us from trying something new, we can tap into that inner courage, which is God's presence, and find our footing. We may still be afraid, but we go forward anyway, knowing we will be given all we need to take on the challenge and tackle any new situation.

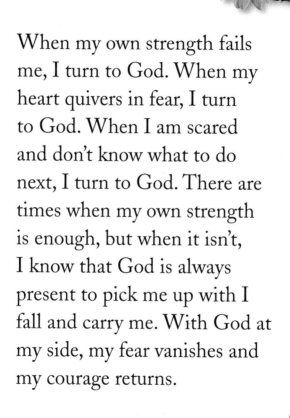

When my own strength fails me, I turn to God. When my heart quivers in fear, I turn to God. When I am scared and don't know what to do next, I turn to God. There are times when my own strength is enough, but when it isn't, I know that God is always present to pick me up with I fall and carry me. With God at my side, my fear vanishes and my courage returns.

Being human means being weak at times, and it is nothing to be ashamed of. Living requires a lot of courage, and when we don't have enough to get us through, we can always turn to one who does. That one is God. Our weakness is his strength, and our fear is his courage. With God, all things are possible and we are always protected, guided, and loved.

I see beauty in kindness,
goodness, and unselfish
grace, in the infinite love
and tenderness of another's
embrace.

Beauty from the heart shines
with a special glow when a
kind and generous spirit resides
inside the soul.

I can do all things through Christ which strengtheneth me.

—Philippians 4:13

In my hours of weakness, I reach out to others for the strength to carry on. In my times of need, I ask for help from others, and their love gives me the courage to keep going. God has given us the gift of other people not just to love us, but also to be there for us when we cannot make it on our own.

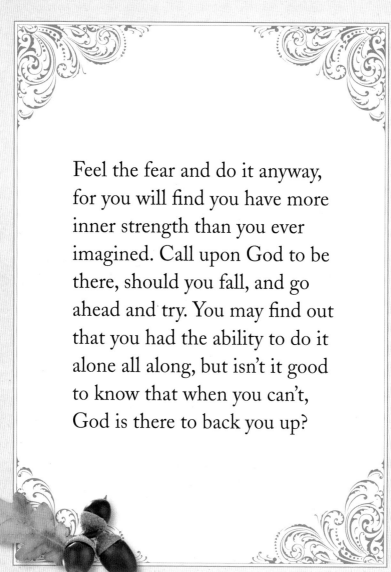

Feel the fear and do it anyway, for you will find you have more inner strength than you ever imagined. Call upon God to be there, should you fall, and go ahead and try. You may find out that you had the ability to do it alone all along, but isn't it good to know that when you can't, God is there to back you up?

November

As thou knowest not what is the way of the spirit, nor how the bones do grow in the womb of her that is with child: even so thou knowest not the works of God who maketh all.

—Ecclesiastes 11:5

When the winds of change and challenge blow hard into my life, I will take refuge in you, O Lord. When the darkness descends upon my house and home, I will fear not for I will place my faith in you, O Lord. When my child is ill or my husband is hurt, I will remain steadfast, for I know that you will be right there by my side, O Lord. Although I cannot see you, I know you are always with me, O Lord, and in that I take comfort and find strength.

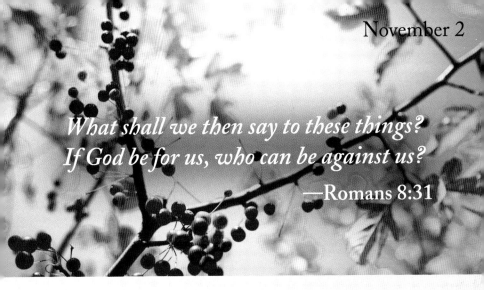

What shall we then say to these things?
If God be for us, who can be against us?
—Romans 8:31

When we are lonely and sad, we forget
that we have a lion within each of us to
call upon. That lion is bold, courageous,
strong, and unafraid. That lion gives us the
extra confidence we need to keep moving,
even when we want to stay still. Listen to
the lion inside and find courage. Then go
forth and roar! God did not make us to
play small and weak.

One of the greatest gifts in life is being able to be there for someone who is suffering. Sharing our strength, hope, and courage with those that are feeling weak is a blessing for all involved. The gift of service in the form of being someone else's pillar of strength, something they can lean on when their own legs fail them, is such a powerful experience of love in action.

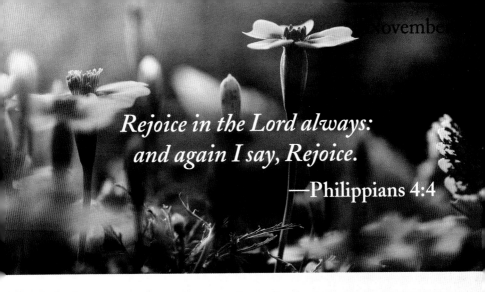

Rejoice in the Lord always:
and again I say, Rejoice.

—Philippians 4:4

There is no greater joy than being able to provide comfort to someone who is going through a rough time. Our love serves to soothe their pain, and our attention allows them to release the weight of their suffering. All we need to do is be there and listen, the way God listens to our prayers and our tears when we need comfort. We can be angels to others in need.

325

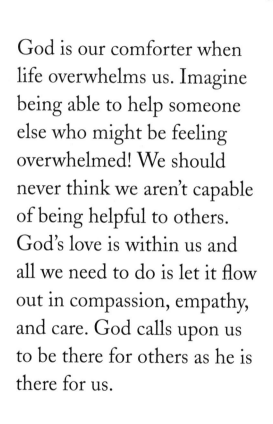

God is our comforter when life overwhelms us. Imagine being able to help someone else who might be feeling overwhelmed! We should never think we aren't capable of being helpful to others. God's love is within us and all we need to do is let it flow out in compassion, empathy, and care. God calls upon us to be there for others as he is there for us.

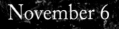

*He that loveth not knoweth not God;
for God is love.*

—1 John 4:8

I know I can count on my friends and family to provide the comfort I need when I am sick or depressed. They do their best to be there, and I return the love and attention. But now and then I need something more. I need God's special brand of comfort and loving care. God's love goes bone-deep and warms the coldest corners of my frightened heart. God's love fills the darkest corners of my broken spirit.

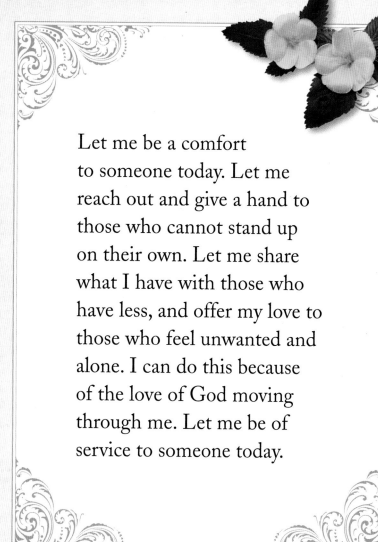

Let me be a comfort to someone today. Let me reach out and give a hand to those who cannot stand up on their own. Let me share what I have with those who have less, and offer my love to those who feel unwanted and alone. I can do this because of the love of God moving through me. Let me be of service to someone today.

Sometimes I hesitate to help someone because I don't know what to say or do. The right words or actions fail me. This is when I turn to God and allow his love to flow through me and express itself as just the right form of comfort the other person needs. It might be a loving hug, or a helping hand, or just sitting with them in silence. God knows best how I can be a comfort to others.

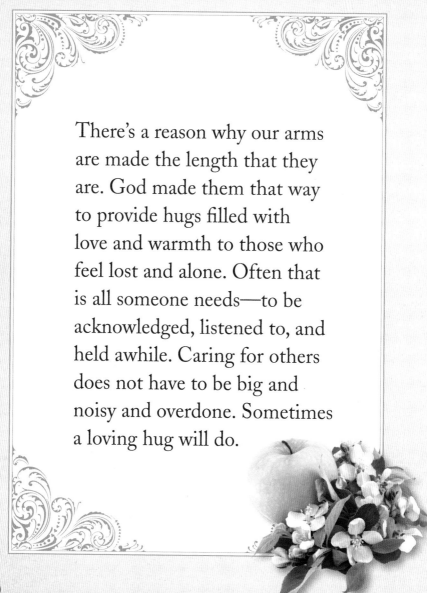

There's a reason why our arms are made the length that they are. God made them that way to provide hugs filled with love and warmth to those who feel lost and alone. Often that is all someone needs—to be acknowledged, listened to, and held awhile. Caring for others does not have to be big and noisy and overdone. Sometimes a loving hug will do.

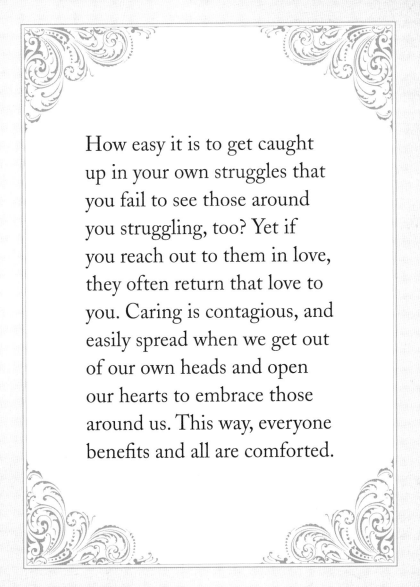

How easy it is to get caught
up in your own struggles that
you fail to see those around
you struggling, too? Yet if
you reach out to them in love,
they often return that love to
you. Caring is contagious, and
easily spread when we get out
of our own heads and open
our hearts to embrace those
around us. This way, everyone
benefits and all are comforted.

One thing have I desired of the Lord,
that will I seek after;
that I may dwell in the house of the Lord
all the days of my life,
to behold the beauty of the Lord,
and to enquire in his temple.

—Psalm 27:4

God is on the job every moment of the
day to give us the comfort we ask for. All
he asks in return is that we give the gift of
that comfort to those we come in contact
with. Sometimes, it's a smile for a stranger,
or a kind word for an old friend. It doesn't
matter how it looks. All that matters is
that we give what we get and let God
perform miracles of kindness through us.

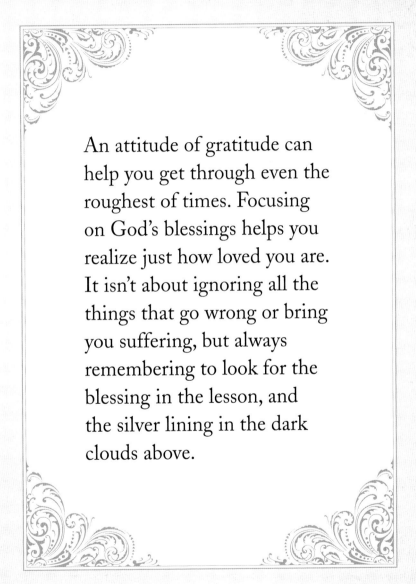

An attitude of gratitude can
help you get through even the
roughest of times. Focusing
on God's blessings helps you
realize just how loved you are.
It isn't about ignoring all the
things that go wrong or bring
you suffering, but always
remembering to look for the
blessing in the lesson, and
the silver lining in the dark
clouds above.

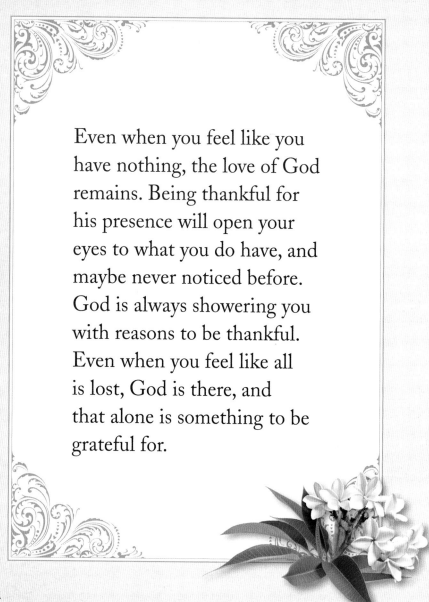

Even when you feel like you
have nothing, the love of God
remains. Being thankful for
his presence will open your
eyes to what you do have, and
maybe never noticed before.
God is always showering you
with reasons to be thankful.
Even when you feel like all
is lost, God is there, and
that alone is something to be
grateful for.

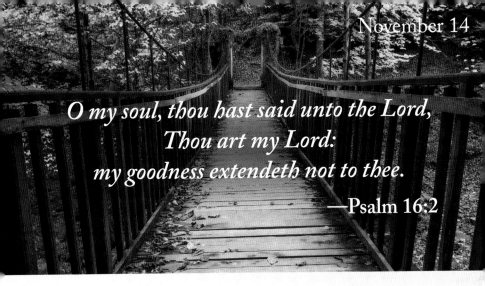

O my soul, thou hast said unto the Lord,
Thou art my Lord:
my goodness extendeth not to thee.

—Psalm 16:2

Give thanks to God, for he is good. Even when we are struggling, God is there to help us. Even when we are feeling lost and alone, God stands beside us and shows us we are loved. Even when we are sure we cannot go on, God picks us up and carries us. Give thanks to God.

Count your blessings and
see how they multiply!
Every challenge teaches
us something we need to
know, which is a blessing.
Every obstacle gives us more
strength, which is a blessing.
Every problem gives us a
chance to stretch our minds
and come up with a new
solution, which is a blessing.
All of the good, and all of the
lessons of the bad, adds up to
an abundance of things to be
grateful for.

I used to take everything in my life for granted. I used to never show gratitude. Then everything was taken away and I suddenly realized what I had all along. Don't let a tragedy or major loss awaken you to the power of being thankful. Do it now. Take nothing for granted, because it can vanish so quickly and it is all a part of being alive, and just to be alive is something to be grateful for.

It's so easy to be thankful for the good. But when we encounter obstacles, how often do we curse them? Yet those difficulties are helping us to evolve into better and stronger and more loving human beings. It's easy to be grateful once the challenges are gone and we are once again in the flow of life. But try to be grateful for the hard times as well. They are very often miracles in disguise.

And thou shalt love the Lord thy God with all thy heart, and with all thy soul, and with all thy mind, and with all thy strength: this is the first commandment.

—Mark 12:30

Wake up in the morning and be grateful for the new day ahead. Every 24 hours is an opportunity to live life more fully, and love more deeply. Look at each moment and see the gift it brings. Cherish the present as it unfolds. Then, when you go to sleep at night, be thankful for the experiences God gave you. This is a life well-lived.

In God is my salvation and my glory:
the rock of my strength, and my refuge, is
in God.

—Psalm 62:7

Holy God, even in times of fear and uncertainty, please remind me that you surround me always. With every breath I take, let me breathe in your merciful love. With every blink of my eyes, let me see your comforting presence. With every beat of my heart, let me feel your spirit envelop me. I ask that you make me yours, totally and completely, and let me rest in the loving refuge of your arms.

Nay, in all these things we are more than conquerors through him that loved us.

—Romans 8:37

We may be surrounded by friends and family, yet still feel so alone and misunderstood. Those around us may have their own problems and worries, leaving us feeling abandoned and unseen. But we are never truly alone, for God is always present. God's love is unceasing and unfailing, and we don't have to ask for it, or wait in line for it. We may forget God, but God never forgets us.

For whoso findeth me findeth life,
and shall obtain favour of the Lord.

—Proverbs 8:35

You never have to walk alone through life, because God walks with you. Whether your path is smooth and free of obstacles, or rough and filled with detours, God is there to help guide you and give you the strength to carry on and keep moving forward. There is no reason to feel lonely, and there is nothing to fear. God is there, now and always.

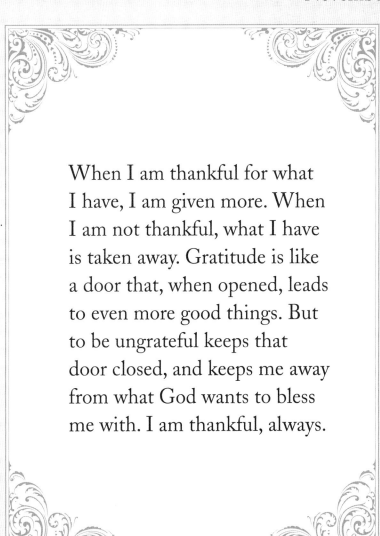

When I am thankful for what I have, I am given more. When I am not thankful, what I have is taken away. Gratitude is like a door that, when opened, leads to even more good things. But to be ungrateful keeps that door closed, and keeps me away from what God wants to bless me with. I am thankful, always.

Heavenly Father, I never fail
to come to you for help and
comfort in the dark times
of my life, yet I don't always
remember you when my cup
is overflowing. Forgive me if I
seem ungrateful and take your
generosity for granted. How
can I forget all that you give
me each day?
You bring beauty, peace,
and love to my existence.
My heart overflows with
thanksgiving.

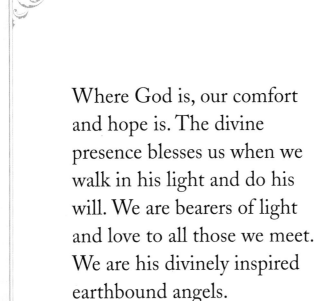

Where God is, our comfort and hope is. The divine presence blesses us when we walk in his light and do his will. We are bearers of light and love to all those we meet. We are his divinely inspired earthbound angels.

Lord, even when the storm is raging all around me, I feel your still, comforting presence. Thank you for letting me know that no matter how dark the skies and regardless of how high the water rises, you are always with me. You meet me in the midst of the storm, wherever you find me, and you calm my troubled spirit. And so, Lord, I praise you in this storm. For in it, I find you.

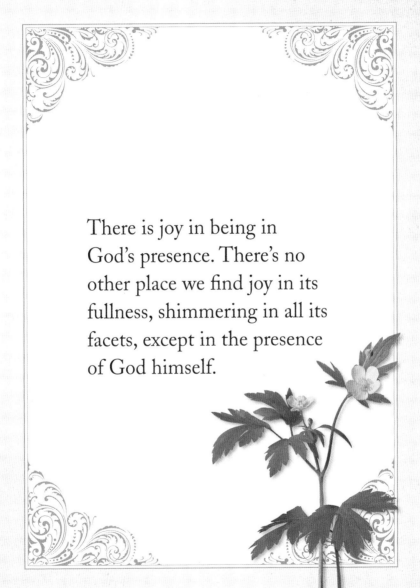

There is joy in being in God's presence. There's no other place we find joy in its fullness, shimmering in all its facets, except in the presence of God himself.

The Bible promises that God will always be with us. Whether we are commuting to work, having coffee with friends, taking a walk, or even sleeping soundly through the night—whatever it is, wherever we are, he's there with us. He's the friend who always has time, never moves to another part of the world, is forever ready to listen, and provides the best counsel. It's just a matter of realizing he's there.

*Know therefore that the Lord thy
God, he is God, the faithful God,
which keepeth covenant and mercy
with them that love him and keep his
commandments to a
thousand generations.*

—Deuteronomy 7:9

Almighty God, why is it we don't
remember that you alone are the source
of all comfort? Thank you for your
faithfulness, Lord. For at the end of every
one of our fruitless searches you are there,
and in your presence we find true comfort.

For my thoughts are not your thoughts,
neither are your ways my ways,
saith the Lord.

—Isaiah 55:8

These nights, these long drawn-out nights
of solitude, are where I find you waiting,
ready to speak comfort to my heart and
assure me that you have a future in store
for me that is good and worth waiting for.
Tonight, even if sleep eludes me again, I'll
continue to rest in your love for me.

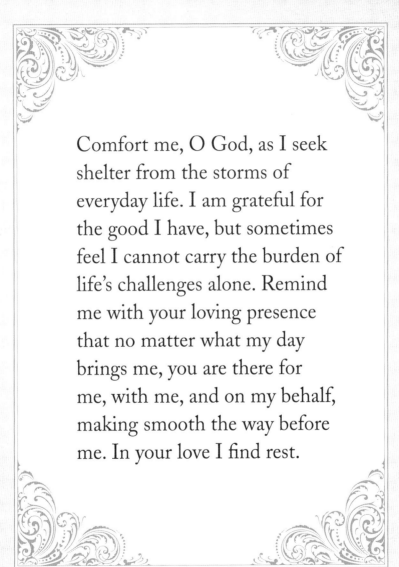

Comfort me, O God, as I seek shelter from the storms of everyday life. I am grateful for the good I have, but sometimes feel I cannot carry the burden of life's challenges alone. Remind me with your loving presence that no matter what my day brings me, you are there for me, with me, and on my behalf, making smooth the way before me. In your love I find rest.

December

As winter's deepest chill,
I cried out for understanding
And to know my Father's
will.
While treading up a garden
path
Hushed in the fragrant air;
I spied a tender rose,
Its petals bowed as if in
prayer.
As I gazed in silent awe,
It occurred to me—he knows!
The tears my Lord has shed
for me
Are the dew upon the rose.

O the depth of the riches both of the wisdom and knowledge of God! how unsearchable are his judgments, and his ways past finding out!

—Romans 11:33

Father, make me resilient like the sandy beach upon which the waves crash. Make me strong like the mighty willow tree that bends but does not break in the high winds. Give me the patience and wisdom to know that my suffering will one day turn to a greater understanding of your ways, your works, and your wonders.

Finally, my brethren, be strong in the Lord, and in the power of his might.

—Ephesians 6:10

Dear Lord, when I am sad, you give me hope. When I am lost, you offer me direction and guidance. When I am alone, you stand beside me. When my heart aches with sorrow, you bring me new blessings. Thank you for your gifts of grace, of love, and of healing. Amen.

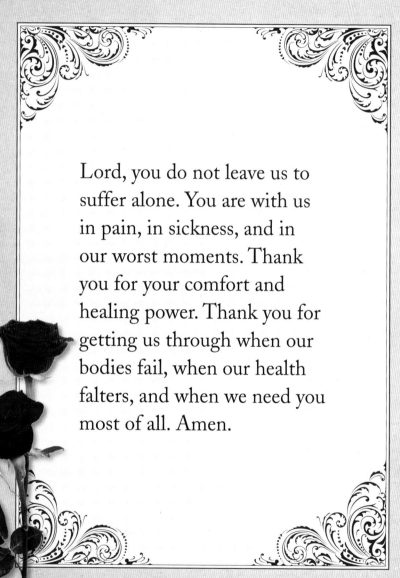

Lord, you do not leave us to suffer alone. You are with us in pain, in sickness, and in our worst moments. Thank you for your comfort and healing power. Thank you for getting us through when our bodies fail, when our health falters, and when we need you most of all. Amen.

*Make thy face to shine upon thy servant:
save me for thy mercies' sake.*

—Psalm 31:16

O God, I know you will never give us a
burden to bear without giving us the grace
to endure it, but some burdens just seem
so heavy we find ourselves wondering if
they can be survived. I ask that you send
an abundant amount of strength and grace
to all those who suffer so. Let them feel
your presence in a very real way, Lord, for
without you, they have no hope. I ask this
in Jesus' name. Amen.

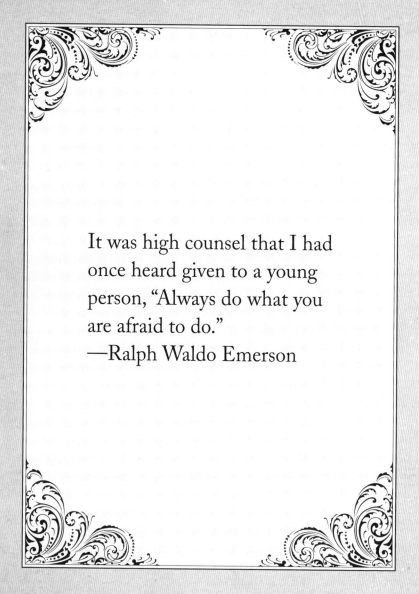

It was high counsel that I had
once heard given to a young
person, "Always do what you
are afraid to do."
—Ralph Waldo Emerson

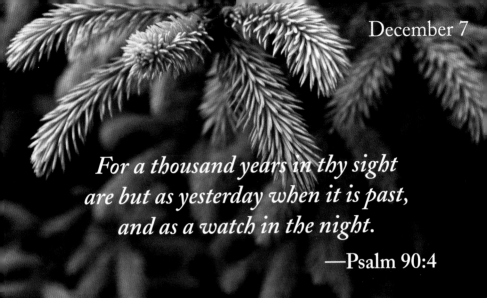

For a thousand years in thy sight
are but as yesterday when it is past,
and as a watch in the night.

—Psalm 90:4

Anyone who has ever been abandoned
deeply fears that they will be abandoned
again. Often the worm of insecurity feeds
the existing fear. It's a cycle of destruction
that has no cure in human relationships.
Even if our loved ones are faithful, still
they are mortal. That's why God's promise
to never leave or forsake us is such a
powerful assurance.

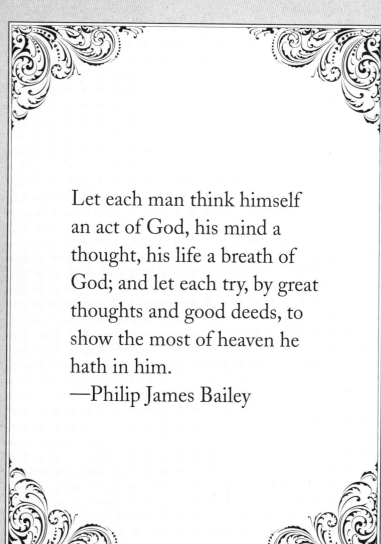

Let each man think himself
an act of God, his mind a
thought, his life a breath of
God; and let each try, by great
thoughts and good deeds, to
show the most of heaven he
hath in him.
—Philip James Bailey

He stumbled, injured,
right leg strong, left folding
down. I watched that green-
headed, curly-tailed drake
hesitate. Then, heeding a hen's
loud call, he hobbled to corn
scattered near a garden wall.
Oh, God, I am injured, too
My sorrows slow to mend.
But today, as I turned from the
mud-room door came the call
of a faithful friend.

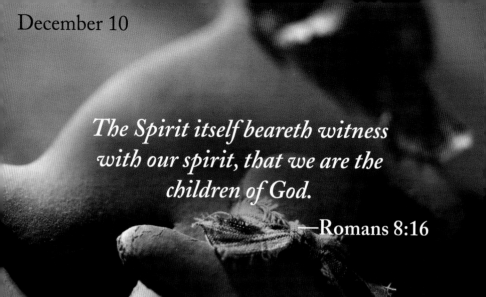

December 10

The Spirit itself beareth witness with our spirit, that we are the children of God.

—Romans 8:16

Earth changes, but thy soul and God stand sure.
—Robert Browning

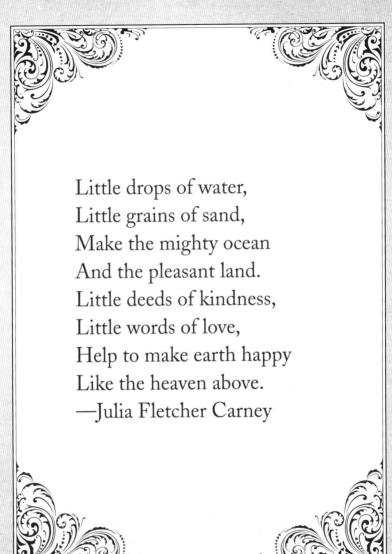

Little drops of water,
Little grains of sand,
Make the mighty ocean
And the pleasant land.
Little deeds of kindness,
Little words of love,
Help to make earth happy
Like the heaven above.
—Julia Fletcher Carney

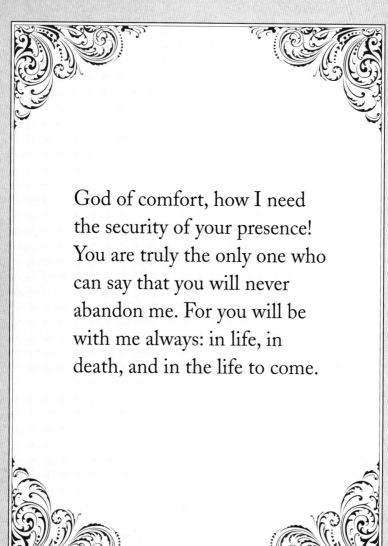

God of comfort, how I need
the security of your presence!
You are truly the only one who
can say that you will never
abandon me. For you will be
with me always: in life, in
death, and in the life to come.

Let every soul be subject unto the higher powers. For there is no power but of God: the powers that be are ordained of God.

—Romans 13:1

I feel an old familiar panic coming over me, Lord. Comfort me now. As I breathe deeply, fill me with the knowledge that you are present and you are in control. Thank you, Lord. Only your intervention can calm my troubled soul.

Lord, you are teaching me that
finding peace requires me to seek
it out—to look for and pursue
peaceful places, peaceful ways,
and peaceful relationships. If I
make living in peace a priority,
I won't miss it, and even when
storms come my way I will know
where to find rest and calm and
quietude of spirit. Your Word
so often pairs righteousness and
peace. To live uprightly is to live
in peace. Help me choose what is
right and true and good today, as
I seek to live in your peace, Lord.

Blessed are they that keep his testimonies, and that seek him with the whole heart.

—Psalm 119:2

Lord, we often think of peace as something that comes when we're ready, when our hands are folded and our minds quiet. But your love and presence are in all things in this world, the loud and the quiet, the raging river as well as the silent pond. You are everywhere, and it is as easy to hear you on a bustling city street as it is in the isolated silence of a redwood forest. Please remind me that I can find your comforting peace anywhere, if my eyes are open and my heart is willing.

The Lord bless thee, and keep thee:
The Lord make his face shine upon thee,
and be gracious unto thee:
The Lord lift up his countenance upon
thee, and give thee peace.

—Numbers 6:24-26

God, your peace is my cornerstone, upon
which I build the foundation of my life.
In your peace, I spread peace to my family
and friends, and to my community, for this
indeed is a world that needs more peace.
Blessed am I to have found that peace in
you, God.

There is a place of total calm
and serenity we can access
at any time. That place is
deep inside of us, where God
dwells in silence as an ever-
present reminder of his love.
In this place, we experience
pure awareness of God's love,
and our spirits are renewed
and refreshed. Even when life
is loud and distracting, we can
come to this peaceful place at
any time.

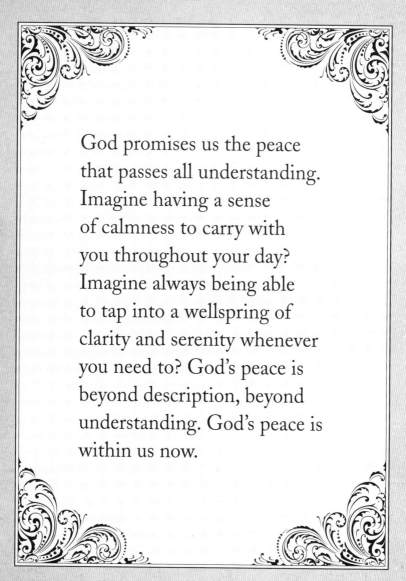

God promises us the peace
that passes all understanding.
Imagine having a sense
of calmness to carry with
you throughout your day?
Imagine always being able
to tap into a wellspring of
clarity and serenity whenever
you need to? God's peace is
beyond description, beyond
understanding. God's peace is
within us now.

Sometimes life overwhelms me and I want to crawl up in a ball and hide away. But responsibilities and obligations do not allow me to, so I turn instead to God for help. He lightens my load and offers me peace, even amidst the coldest days and nights. He takes my difficulties away, and replaces them with strength and resilience. When I turn to God, I am at peace and in the flow of his will for me.

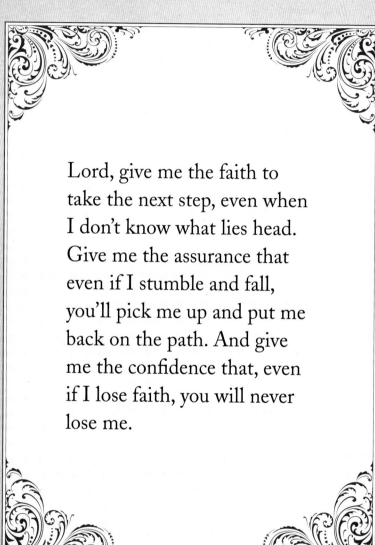

Lord, give me the faith to take the next step, even when I don't know what lies head. Give me the assurance that even if I stumble and fall, you'll pick me up and put me back on the path. And give me the confidence that, even if I lose faith, you will never lose me.

It is he that buildeth his stories in the heaven,
and hath founded his troop in the earth;
he that calleth for the waters of the sea,
and poureth them out upon the face of the
earth: The Lord is his name.

—Amos 9:6

Come, ye disconsolate, where'er ye
languish;
come, at the shrine of God fervently kneel;
here bring your wounded hearts; here tell
your anguish;
earth has no sorrow that heaven
cannot heal.
—Thomas Moore

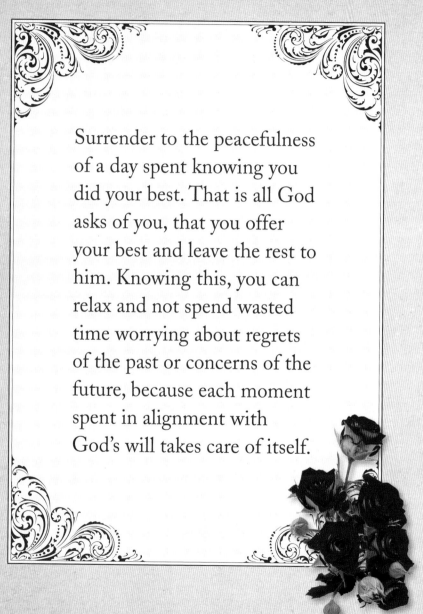

Surrender to the peacefulness
of a day spent knowing you
did your best. That is all God
asks of you, that you offer
your best and leave the rest to
him. Knowing this, you can
relax and not spend wasted
time worrying about regrets
of the past or concerns of the
future, because each moment
spent in alignment with
God's will takes care of itself.

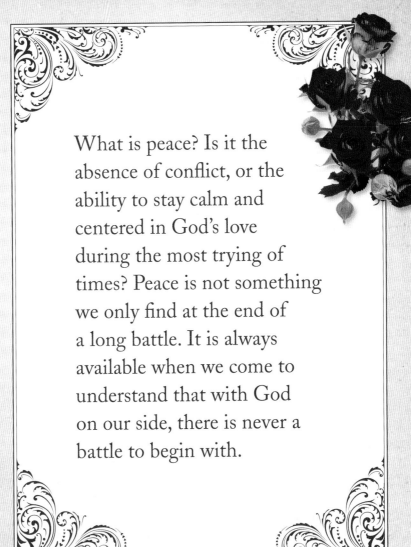

What is peace? Is it the absence of conflict, or the ability to stay calm and centered in God's love during the most trying of times? Peace is not something we only find at the end of a long battle. It is always available when we come to understand that with God on our side, there is never a battle to begin with.

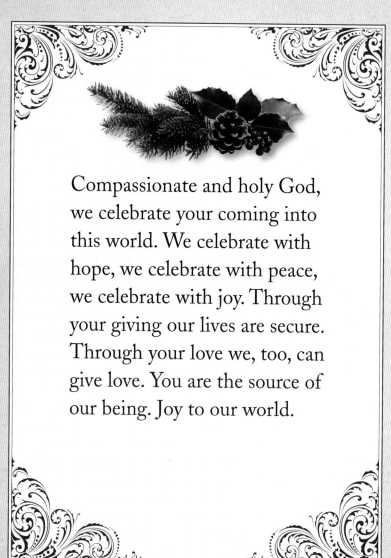

Compassionate and holy God, we celebrate your coming into this world. We celebrate with hope, we celebrate with peace, we celebrate with joy. Through your giving our lives are secure. Through your love we, too, can give love. You are the source of our being. Joy to our world.

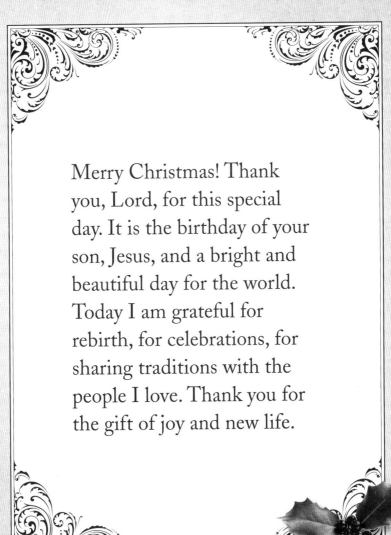

Merry Christmas! Thank you, Lord, for this special day. It is the birthday of your son, Jesus, and a bright and beautiful day for the world. Today I am grateful for rebirth, for celebrations, for sharing traditions with the people I love. Thank you for the gift of joy and new life.

Father in heaven, when all
else fails, I turn to you for the
comfort only you can provide.
I have done all I can do, and
now I rest in the belief that
you are taking from me my
burdens and doing for me what
I cannot. In you alone do I find
that comforting assurance that
everything is being taken care
of and that all will work out as
it should. My surrender to your
comfort is not out of weakness
but out of my faith in your
eternal love and concern for me.
For that I am grateful.

Living with stress causes
so many health problems,
not to mention strain on
your mental and emotional
state. Perhaps you cannot
remove everything in life
that causes you stress, but
you can approach it with
a sense of inner peace that
makes you unshakeable and
unstoppable. Life will never
be perfectly calm, but as long
as you are within, where God
lives and moves and has his
being, it won't matter what is
happening on the outside.

For I know the thoughts that I think toward you, saith the Lord, thoughts of peace, and not of evil, to give you an expected end.

—Jeremiah 29:11

The sting of rejection lingers long after it has been inflicted. It often creates an aversion to drawing near to the very thing that can bring healing: love through a relationship with God. It takes a certain willingness to risk reaching out to be forgiven by God if we ever hope to find wholeness again. But there is no more worthwhile risk than that which risks for the sake of God's love.

O Lord Almighty, what
comfort I find in your
constancy and faithfulness.
You are the same God who
hung the stars in the universe
and called them by name.
You've heard the prayers
of troubled souls since the
beginning of time, and yet
you never stop listening.
Thank you, Lord, for your
constant sovereignty and your
unfailing love. You are indeed
our comfort and our strength
when all about us seems to be
falling apart.

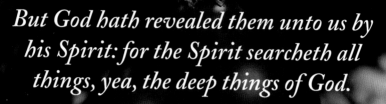

December 30

But God hath revealed them unto us by his Spirit: for the Spirit searcheth all things, yea, the deep things of God.

—1 Corinthians 2:10

God's peace is a bone-deep peace that calms every cell of the body. God's peace is a powerful peace that stops the storms within and without, and gently calls the spirit home to shore. God's peace is a comforting peace that soothes the heart-wounds whole again. God's peace is a bone-deep peace that quiets the restless soul.

I can count on God to be
there for me through thick and
thin, good days and bad days,
laughter and tears, joy and
despair. No matter what I am
experiencing, God is there to
comfort me and help me, and
even to point out the lessons I
was meant to learn along the
way. I can count on people to
be there for me some of the
time, but only God is reliable
24 hours a day, 7 days a week,
365 days a year.